KNOTS
STEP BY STEP

KNOTS
STEP BY STEP

DES PAWSON

LONDON
Project Editor Ed Wilson
Project Art Editor Keith Davis
Production Editor Ben Marcus
Production Controller
Mandy Inness
Jacket Designer Silke Spingies
Managing Editor
Stephanie Farrow
Managing Art Editor Lee Griffiths
Photography Sam Scott-Hunter,
Tim Pestridge

DELHI
Senior Editor Nidhi Sharma
Editor Pallavi Singh
Designers Simran Kaur,
Vikas Sachdeva, Kanika Mittal
DTP Designer Shanker Prasad
DTP Manager Balwant Singh
Managing Art Editor
Romi Chakraborty
Managing Editor Saloni Talwar

This edition published in 2022
First published in Great Britain
in 2012 by
Dorling Kindersley Limited,
One Embassy Gardens,
8 Viaduct Gardens,
London, SW11 7BW

Copyright © 2012, 2022
Dorling Kindersley Limited
A Penguin Random House
Company
10 9 8 7 6 5 4 3 2 1
001–322078–Jan/2022

A CIP catalogue record for this
book is available from the British
Library.

ISBN: 978-0-2414-7121-0
Printed and bound in China

For the curious
www.dk.com

Contents

6 Introduction
7 About This Book

GETTING STARTED
10 Rope Construction
12 Rope Materials
14 Rope Maintenance
16 Storing Rope
18 Terms and Tools
20 Techniques

STOPPER KNOTS
28 Overhand Knot
30 Slipped Overhand Knot
32 Double Overhand Knot
34 Best for... Sailing
38 Figure of Eight
40 Slipped Figure of Eight
42 Stopper Knot
44 Sink Stopper Knot
47 Stevedore Knot
49 Monkey's Fist
54 Crown Knot
56 Wall Knot
58 Matthew Walker Knot
61 Manrope Knot
72 Diamond Knot

BINDING KNOTS
80 True Lover's Knot
82 Sailor's Cross
85 Reef Knot
87 Slipped Reef Knot
90 Slipped Reef Knot Doubled
92 Granny Knot
94 Thief Knot
96 Surgeon's Knot
98 Surgeon's Knot with
      Second Tuck
99 Turquoise Turtle
102 Packer's Knot
105 Clove Hitch
107 Clove Hitch –
      Second Method
109 Constrictor Knot
111 Timber Hitch
114 Boa Knot
117 Turk's Head – Three-Lead
      Four-Bight
124 Best for... Household
128 Turk's Head – Four-Lead
      Five-Bight
133 Turk's Head – Five-Lead
      Four-Bight

BENDS

140 Sheet Bend
142 Tucked Sheet Bend
144 Double Sheet Bend
146 Rope Yarn Knot
148 Carrick Bend
150 Hunter's Bend
152 Lanyard Knot
155 Ashley's Bend
157 Fisherman's Knot
160 Double Fisherman's Knot
164 Best for... Climbing
168 Blood Knot
172 Water Knot

HITCHES

176 Rolling Hitch
178 Mirrored Rolling Hitch
180 Round Turn & Two
    Half Hitches
182 Buntline Hitch
184 Fisherman's Bend
186 Best for... Camping
190 Cow Hitch
191 Pedigree Cow Hitch
192 Cow Hitch with Toggle
194 Sheepshank
196 Sheepshank Man o' War
199 Marlinespike Hitch
201 Highwayman's Hitch
203 Waggoner's Hitch
205 Snelling a Hook
207 Clinch Knot
208 Improved Clinch Knot
209 Palomar Knot
211 Square Lashing
215 Diagonal Lashing
218 Best for... Gardening
222 Sheer Lashing
225 Icicle Hitch
228 Prusik Knot
230 Bachmann Knot
232 Klemheist Knot
234 Italian Hitch
235 Reversed Italian Hitch

LOOPS

238 Alpine Butterfly
240 Bowline
242 Bowline – Second Method
245 Bowline with Two Turns

248 Bowline with Stopper
249 Figure-of-Eight Loop
251 Threaded Figure-of-Eight
    Loop
253 Overhand Loop
255 Double Overhand Loop
257 Double Overhand
    Sliding Loop
259 Bowline on the Bight
262 Portuguese Bowline
265 Spanish Bowline
267 Angler's Loop
269 Single Figure-of-Eight
    Loop on the Bight
271 Englishman's Loop
273 Double Englishman's Loop
274 Best for...Fishing
278 Blood Dropper Knot
280 Bimini Twist
283 Basic Net
285 Cargo Net Knot
287 Jury Mast Knot

PLAITS & SENNITS

292 Three-Strand Flat Plait
294 Four-Strand Flat Plait
296 Five-Strand Flat Plait
298 Six-Strand Flat Plait
300 Seven-Strand Flat Plait
302 Best for... Gifts
306 Ocean-Plait Mat
311 Oval Mat
316 Chain Sennit
319 Four-Strand Round Sennit
321 Eight-Strand Square Sennit
324 Round Crown Sennit
327 Six-Strand Round Crowning
330 Square Crown Sennit

SPLICES & WHIPPINGS

334 Back Splice
342 Eye Splice
347 Short Splice
364 Tapering a Splice
370 Best for... Horses
374 Common Whipping
376 French Whipping
379 Sailmaker's Whipping
383 Palm & Needle Whipping
387 Seizing
390 Stitch & Seize

394 Glossary
396 Index
400 Acknowledgments

Introduction

Knots have been used throughout history, and they remain a valuable resource today. Learning to tie knots is a handy, enjoyable skill, requiring only simple equipment to get started.

This book contains a selection of knots intended to be practical and instructive. Many of them have specific purposes, others are purely decorative, while some can be used for many different tasks; all of them should be reliable and safe if tied correctly. You will find them useful in everyday life as well as in activities such as climbing, sailing, and camping.

As with any skill, it is best to begin by learning the basics. Familiarize yourself with the fundamental techniques, the different types of rope and their uses, and a few technical terms. Use the rope attached to this book to experiment with some simple knots before you attempt anything complicated; classic knots such as the Reef Knot (*see pp.85–86*) and the Overhand Knot (*see pp.28–29*) are both excellent places to begin.

When learning to tie new knots, don't rush – pause regularly to make adjustments as needed and above all, have fun!

Des Pawson

About this Book

Read the brief description at the start of each chapter to work out which type of knot you need, then use the icons and text at the beginning of each knot to refine your search. Once you have found the knot you are looking for, follow the step-by-step instructions to learn how it is tied. This book also contains information on rope and tools, and the best knots for activities such as sailing and climbing.

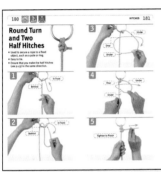

Step-by-step knot sequence
Opening with an overview of the function and characteristics of the knot, these pages use step-by-step photography, accompanied by clear instructions, to demonstrate how the knot is tied.

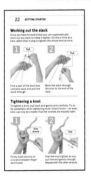

Getting started
This section outlines the equipment and basic techniques needed to tie the knots featured in this book.

Best for...
These feature pages profile the six best knots for specific activities such as gardening or fishing.

Icons

The activities for which each knot can be used are indicated by these icons:

 General

 Fishing

 Climbing

 Sailing

 Camping

 Decorative

Getting Started

Using the correct type of rope for a particular task is key to tying knots effectively. This chapter details how the properties of rope vary according to its construction and composition, with useful advice on storage and maintenance and a range of basic terms and techniques.

Rope Construction

The rope-making process involves fibre being spun into yarn. The yarn is then twisted into large strands or braided, sometimes around a core. The qualities of a rope are partly determined by this process.

Three-strand rope

Rope with three strands is made by twisting fibres into yarns, then twisting the yarns together into strands. Three of the strands are then twisted into rope. At each stage the direction of the twist is opposite to that of the stage before: this creates the friction that holds all the strands together.

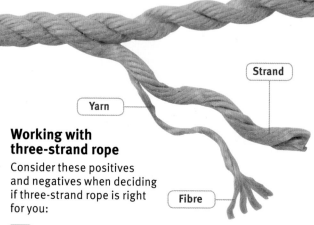

Strand

Yarn

Fibre

Working with three-strand rope

Consider these positives and negatives when deciding if three-strand rope is right for you:

✓ Firm and flexible.

✓ Easy to splice (*see pp.334–63*).

✓ Perfect for rigging traditional sailing vessels.

✓ A good choice for decorative knotting.

✗ Strands will untwist unless the ends are whipped (*see p.14*) to stop them from fraying.

✗ Kinks easily while being coiled.

✗ May have too much stretch for some tasks.

Braided rope

The most common type of this rope has a braided cover with a core of woven or twisted yarn made from synthetic fibres. The fibres in the core and the cover are not always the same. Many braided ropes are developed for specialized purposes.

Core

Cover

Working with braided rope

Consider these positives and negatives when deciding if braided rope is right for you:

✓ Has a smooth feel and good flexibility.

✓ Suitable for a variety of purposes.

✓ Has less stretch and less tendency to kink than three-strand rope.

✓ Reliable in situations where safety is paramount, such as mountaineering and climbing.

✗ Difficult to splice. Some braided rope cannot be spliced at all.

Fishing Line

- Fishing line is usually thin and slippery – you may need to use special knots, often with many turns (see p.274), when working with it.

- To help bed the turns into place, moisten the line prior to working it tight. This will make the knot difficult to untie.

Multiple turns

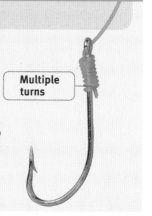

Rope Materials

Until the second half of the 20th century all rope was made from natural plant fibres. Since then, however, synthetic fibres have taken over, and now most rope is manufactured from synthetic materials.

Natural rope

The most common natural fibres in use today are cotton, sisal, and manila. They are aesthetically pleasing but tend to decay quickly and wear out faster than synthetic fibres.

Cotton

Fibres of cotton grow around the seeds of the plant. They can be used to make soft, smooth ropes.

- Stretchy and soft to touch.

- Used mainly for decorative purposes.

- Commonly used for animal halters.

Sisal

Fibres of sisal are stiff and come from the agave plant.

- Inexpensive and fairly coarse.

- Holds knots well.

- Can be treated with a waterproofing agent, making it suitable for exposure to moisture.

Manila

Fibres of manila come from the abaca plant.

- One of the strongest natural ropes.

- Less susceptible to decay than sisal and cotton.

Synthetic rope

Synthetic fibres are stronger than natural fibres and are resistant to decay. The most common synthetics used for making rope are polypropylene, polyester, and nylon. Racing Yachts may also use exotics such as Kevlar, Dyneema®, and HMPE (beyond the scope of this book).

Polypropylene

Polypropylene is low-cost and varied in form.

- Has a tendency to break down in sunlight – needs to be treated against ultraviolet rays.

- More liable to chafe than other synthetic fibres.

- Floats in water.

- Slightly slippery – needs to be tied with a secure knot.

Polyester

Polyester is one of the best ropes for outdoor use.

- Wears well – resistant to chafing and sunlight.

- As strong as nylon but has less stretch.

- Can be purchased pre-stretched, meaning there will be minimal stretch during use.

Nylon

Nylon fibres were the first synthetic material to be used for making rope.

- Has a degree of stretch – particularly good for absorbing shock loads.

- Good for making ropes used for mooring boats and climbing.

- Tends to stiffen over time.

- Resists the ultraviolet rays in sunlight better than polypropylene, but not as well as polyester.

Rope Maintenance

Good rope maintenance will preserve the strength of a
rope and increase its life span. If the rope is being used for
activities that carry an element of risk, such as climbing or
abseiling, rope maintenance is an essential safety procedure.

Binding ends

Unless they are bound in a process called whipping, the
ends of three-strand and braided rope will unravel and
fray. The ends of a rope can be finished with either a
temporary whippingor a permanent twine whipping.

Permanent whipping

Bear in mind the following
points when making a
permanent whipping:

- Whipping should be at
least one and a half times
the diameter of the rope.

Whipping twine

- A Common Whipping
(*see pp.374–75*) is quick
to make and suitable for
three-strand and braided
rope.

- The Sailmaker's Whipping
(*see pp.379–82*) is suitable
for three-strand rope.

- For braided rope, a Palm
and Needle Whipping (*see
pp.383–86*) is used to bind
the core and cover together.

Temporary whipping

If there is not enough time to
make a permanent whipping,
a temporary whipping can
be used. The following
methods are all suitable
for making a temporary
whipping:

Self-adhesive tape

- Self-adhesive tape
wrapped around the rope.

- A Constrictor Knot
(*see pp.109–10*) tied
with thin twine.

- A small amount of
quick-drying glue applied
to the end of the rope.

- Melting the end of synthetic
rope. Be careful to avoid
burning your fingers.

Rope care

Ropes should be kept free from wear and tear, such as chafing caused by constant rubbing of the fibres against hard or rough surfaces.

Looking after rope

The following tips will help you to keep your rope in good condition:

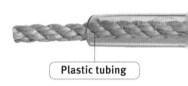

Plastic tubing

■ To prevent chafing, fix some plastic tubing (*see right*) over parts of the rope that are in constant contact with a rough surface.

■ If the rope does become worn, avoid putting it under any strain.

■ Clean dirty rope with a scrubbing brush (*see left*), using water and washing-up liquid. Afterwards, coil the rope (*see pp.16–17*) and hang it up to dry.

■ Rope made from natural fibres should never be stored when it is wet because it will quickly decay.

Brush the rope

Rope deterioration

■ Worn or broken yarns or fibres sticking out from a rope are signs of deterioration.

■ Untwist the lay of the rope to see if grit or sand are causing hidden damage.

■ Rope that shows signs of deterioration should not be used for any tasks or activities that may involve risk to a person or property.

Worn yarns

Storing Rope

When you are not working with your rope, coil it up neatly to prevent it from becoming tangled and then hang it in a dry place. Make sure natural-fibre rope is completely dry before you store it away.

Coiling rope

Coil rope carefully into loops with even turns that follow the twists of the rope's construction. Use some thin line to hold the loops together so the coiling cannot be disturbed.

Braided rope

Coil braided rope into figure-of-eight loops to balance the left- and right-hand twists of its strands.

Three-strand rope

Coil three-strand rope into loops in a clockwise direction.

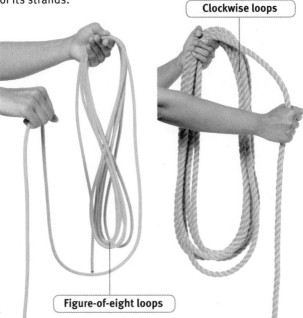

Clockwise loops

Figure-of-eight loops

Making a self-stopped coil

The working end of a rope can be used to make a stopper that holds the coils together. The stopper can then be used to hang up the rope.

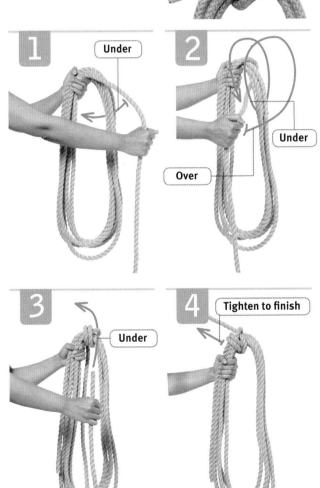

Terms and Tools

To tie the knots in this book, all you need to know
are a few important terms, and how to use certain
specialist tools that will help you with some of
the more complex tasks.

Ends of the rope

The end of the rope that you actively use to make a knot
is called the working end. The other end is inactive and
is known as the standing part.

Working end

Standing part

Shaping the rope

You can bend a rope into shapes such as a bight, loop, and
crossing turn, to help create different knots.

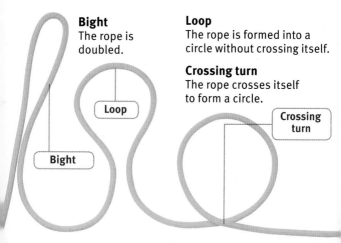

Bight
The rope is
doubled.

Loop
The rope is formed into a
circle without crossing itself.

Crossing turn
The rope crosses itself
to form a circle.

Loop

Crossing
turn

Bight

Turns around an object

When you pass the working end of a rope around another rope, or around an object, the manoeuvre is described as making a turn.

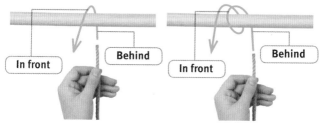

In front **Behind** **In front** **Behind**

Turn
A turn is a single pass of the rope around an object. It is also known as a single turn.

Round turn
A round turn is two turns, or passing the rope twice, around the object.

Useful tools

A few simple but specialized tools will help to make working with rope considerably easier. These tools are available from chandlery stores or on the Internet.

Sailmaker's palm and needle
A reinforced glove and heavy needle. The glove makes it easier to push the needle through thick rope.

Adhesive tape
For quick, temporary whippings.

Sharp knife
Essential for cutting or trimming rope.

Swedish fid
The hollow blade makes it easier to tuck rope when splicing.

Marlinespike
An all-metal tool used for separating the strands of a knot.

Netting needle
For working with thin line when making nets.

Techniques

Some basic knot-tying techniques will provide you with the fundamental skills to make both simple and complicated knots in a quick and easy fashion.

Estimating rope length

To estimate how much rope is needed for a knot make a dummy with loose turns, leaving out the actual tucks. It is better to over-estimate how much rope is required rather than run out of cord.

Loose turns

Working with a long length of rope

More complex knots will require a long length of rope. Rather than attempting to manipulate an unwieldy working end, simply form a bight (*see p.18*).

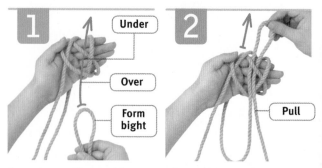

1 Under / Over / Form bight

2 Pull

Form the working end into a bight by folding it back on itself before tucking.

After tucking the bight, pull the rest of the working end through.

Unlaying and laying rope

Some knots and most splices (*see pp.334–63*) are made with the strands of the rope, rather than the whole rope. You can unlay these by opening them up or lay them to remake the rope.

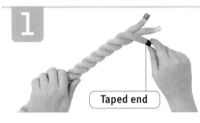

Unlaying a rope

Tape the end of each strand as you unlay it, making sure you keep the twist in the strand intact.

Taped end

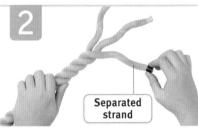

Separate the strands by gently untwisting each one from the body of the rope.

Separated strand

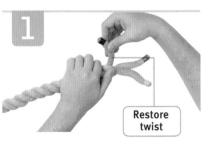

Laying a rope

When relaying an unlaid piece of rope, try to restore the original twist in each strand to hold them together.

Restore twist

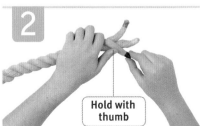

Force the strand into place with your thumb before moving on to the next strand.

Hold with thumb

Working out the slack

Once you have formed a knot you can systematically work out any slack to make it tighter. Do this a little at a time rather than trying to tighten the whole knot at once.

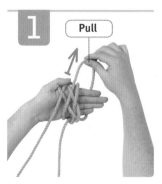

Find a part of the knot that contains slack and pull the slack through.

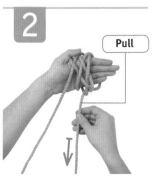

Work the slack through the knot to the end of the rope.

Tightening a knot

To tighten a knot, pull each end gently and carefully. Try to be systematic when tightening multi-strand knots – an even knot can only be created if all the strands are equally tight.

Firmly hold one end of a strand between finger and thumb.

Feel the knot tighten as you pull the end gently through. Repeat with the other strands.

Forming a half hitch

A half hitch is a simple manoeuvre that is one of the building blocks of knot tying. Usually, half hitches are made around an object, such as a pole, or another rope.

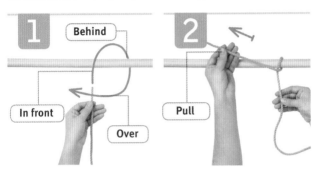

Make a half hitch by taking the rope once around the object you are securing it to.

Lock the half hitch in place by passing one end of the rope across the other end.

Forming a crossing turn

A crossing turn, like a half hitch, is the basis of many knots. It can be formed by rolling the rope between the finger and thumb of one hand so that it twists over or under itself to form a loop.

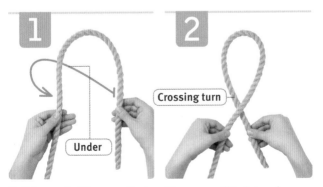

Roll the part of the rope that is to lie under the turn between the thumb and fingers.

The rope will twist under itself to form the crossing turn.

Doubling up

Knots can often be doubled – or even tripled – by replicating the original pattern with additional strands. These should follow the path of the first strand without crossing it.

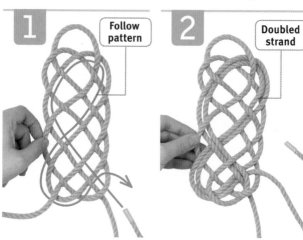

Create the first pattern of the knot, making sure there is enough space for the second pass. Follow around with the second strand.

Ensure that the doubling strand does not cross the original strand. Some knots can be tripled or even quadrupled.

Trimming the ends

Trim ends

When you have finished a knot, a splice, or a whipping, you will probably have some loose ends. Cut off these surplus ends with a sharp knife.

Not too close

Do not trim an end too close to the body of the knot or the splice, as it may pull out when put under strain.

Working into shape

A knot will probably need to be coaxed into a neat and even shape. This process is known as dressing a knot. A knot that is tidy is likely to be stronger and more secure.

Working with your fingers and thumbs, push and pull the strands into shape. Turns may need to be twisted tight.

Ensure the strands of the rope sit neatly alongside each other, emphasizing the knot's structure and increasing effectiveness.

Seizing

Seizing involves using small line to bind together two parts of a larger rope or two or more larger ropes positioned side by side. Historically, the fixed rigging on sailing ships were seized rather than knotted or spliced together.

Stopper Knots

Stopper knots are used to stop a rope fraying or unravelling, or to prevent it from being pulled through a hole or block. Some stopper knots are tied with just the strands of the rope, but most are tied with the whole rope.

Overhand Knot

- The simplest of all knots.
- The basis of knots in the bend and loop families.
- Difficult to untie when tightened.
- Also known as the Thumb Knot.

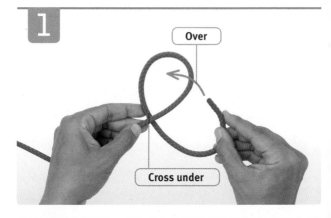

Over

Cross under

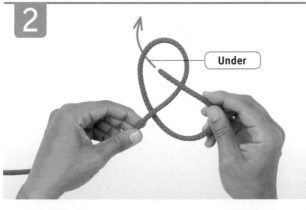

Under

3

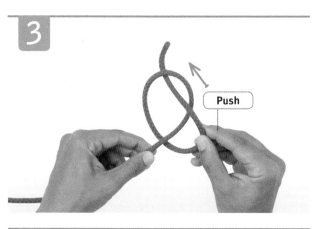

Push

4

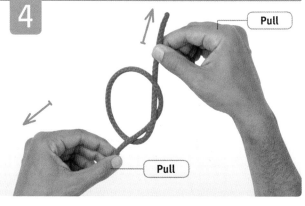

Pull

Pull

5

Tighten to finish

Slipped Overhand Knot

- A simple slipknot that can be tied in the middle or at the end of the rope.
- Easier to untie than the Overhand Knot (*see pp.28–29*).
- Untie by pulling on the short end of the loop.

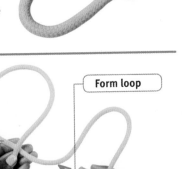

1

Cross under

Form loop

2

Over

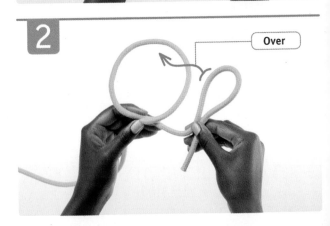

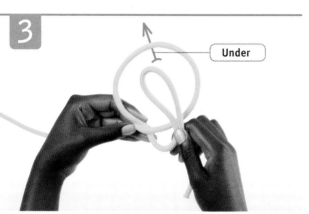

3

Under

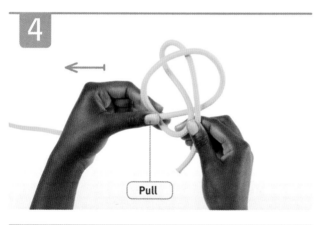

4

Pull

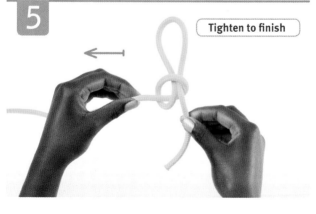

5

Tighten to finish

Double Overhand Knot

- A secure stopper knot that is difficult to untie.
- Bulkier than the Overhand Knot (*see pp.28–29*).
- Can be made larger by adding extra turns.

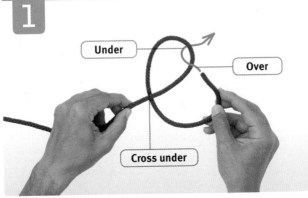

1

Under

Over

Cross under

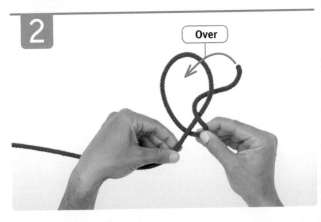

2

Over

3

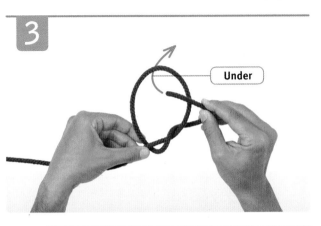

Under

4

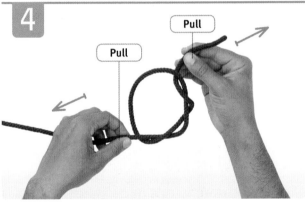

Pull

Pull

5

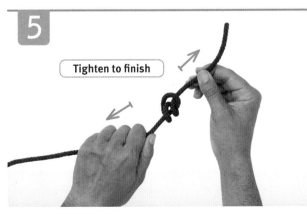

Tighten to finish

BEST FOR ...
Sailing

A good sailor only needs to know how to tie half a dozen basic knots. These knots will help to secure and control the lines, halyards, lanyards, painters, and sheets on yachts, dinghies, and other boats.

Bowline » pp.240–41

✓ A versatile knot – the Bowline is often called the king of all loop knots.

✓ Easy to tie and untie, so is ideal for tying lanyards to fenders, sheets to sails, and making a loop to throw over a bollard.

✗ Difficult to untie under strain and can loosen when not under load.

Similar knots:
» pp.246–47 Bowline with Two Turns
» p.248 Bowline with Stopper

Figure of Eight
» pp.38–39

✓ A stopper knot with some bulk that is quick to tie.

✓ Ideal for stopping the end of a rope from running out through a block.

✓ An easy knot to untie, even if it has been under a lot of strain.

Similar knots:
» pp.44–46 Sink Stopper Knot
» pp.47–48 Stevedore Knot

Sheet Bend »pp.140–41

✅ A quick and easy method of joining two ropes together.

✅ A Double Sheet Bend can be used to tie ropes of different diameters together securely.

❌ Not suitable for joining ropes of different sizes.

Similar knots:
» pp.142–43 Tucked Sheet Bend
» pp.144–45 Double Sheet Bend

Round Turn and Two Half Hitches »pp.180–81

✅ Perfect for tying a rope to a mooring post or ring, as the round turn takes much of the strain off the rope.

✅ Can be untied easily, even when it is under strain.

✅ The pull of the rope can be at right angles to the ring or post to which it is attached.

Similar knots:
» pp.184–85 Fisherman's Bend

Rolling Hitch
» pp.176–77

✅ Can be used to tie a
second line to a sheet
in order to relieve strain.

✅ Useful for tying a
fender lanyard to a rail.

❌ Can fail if the pull
of the lines are not
properly aligned.

Similar knots:
**» pp.178–79
Mirrored
Rolling Hitch**

Reef Knot **» pp.85–86**

✅ Ideal for tying up a
bundle of material.

✅ Can also be used to
fasten the unused part
of a sail around the mast.

✅ Can be slipped for
quick release.

❌ Not suitable for joining two
ropes together – it may
collapse and come undone.

Similar knots:
**» pp.87–88
Slipped Reef Knot
» pp.96–98
Surgeon's Knot**

Figure of Eight

- Used to prevent a rope from slipping through a hole.
- This knot structure is the basis for several other knots such as the Packer's Knot (*see pp.102–04*).
- Can be tied quickly and untied easily.
- Works well as the base of a loop knot.

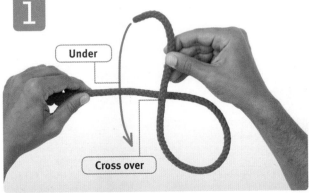

Under

Cross over

2

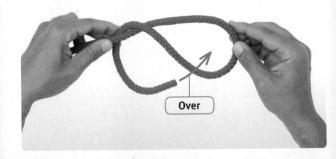

Over

3

Under

4

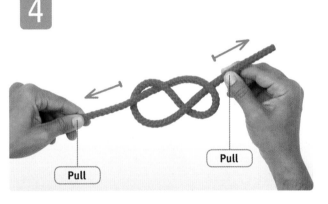

Pull

Pull

5

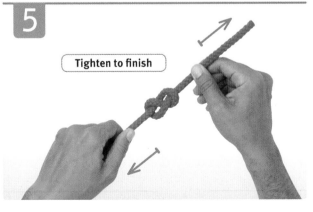

Tighten to finish

Slipped Figure of Eight

- A stopper knot that is quick to tie.
- Easier to untie than the Figure of Eight (*see pp.38–39*).
- Ensure that you work the knot tight so it does not come undone inadvertently.

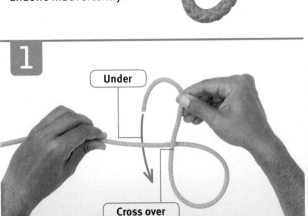

1

Under

Cross over

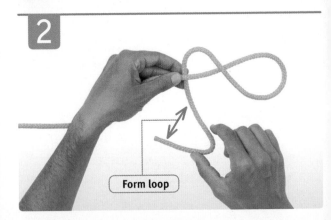

2

Form loop

3

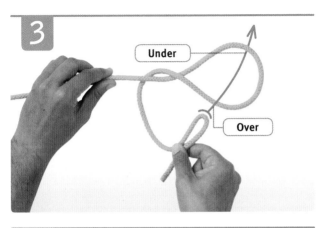

Under

Over

4

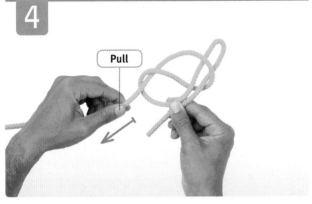

Pull

5

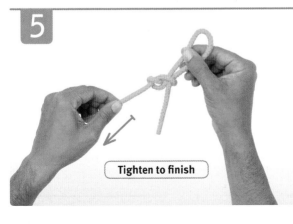

Tighten to finish

Stopper Knot

- Gives weight to the end of a rope that needs to be thrown.
- A variation of the Overhand Knot (*see pp.28–29*) and one of the most decorative stopper knots.

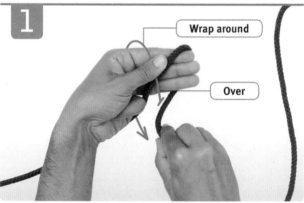

1

Wrap around

Over

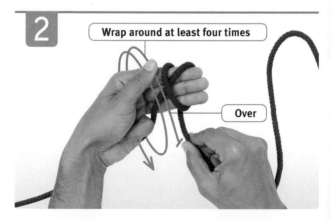

2

Wrap around at least four times

Over

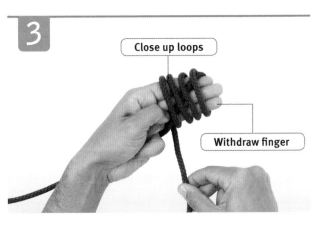

3

Close up loops

Withdraw finger

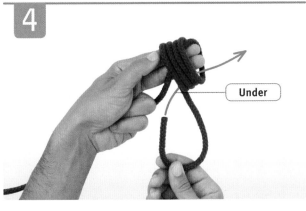

4

Under

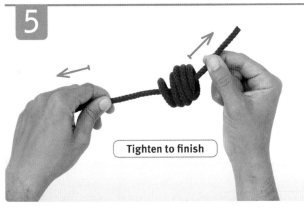

5

Tighten to finish

Sink Stopper Knot

- Used to prevent a thin rope from slipping through a large hole.
- Needs to be carefully tightened and worked into shape.
- Difficult to untie when tightened.

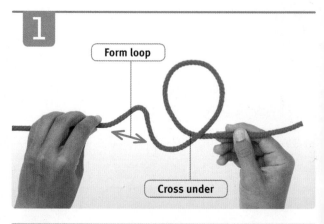

1

Form loop

Cross under

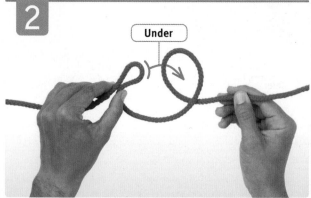

2

Under

3

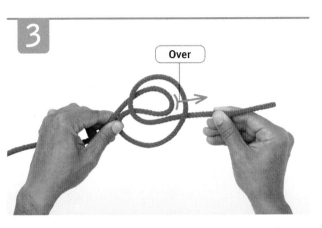

Over

4

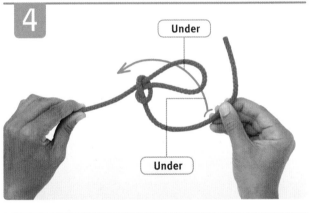

Under

Under

5

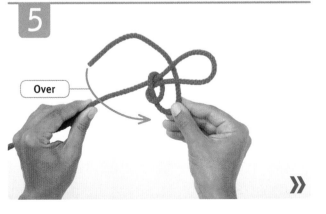

Over

»

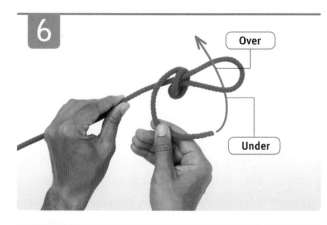

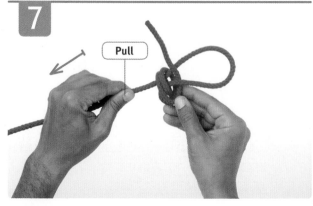

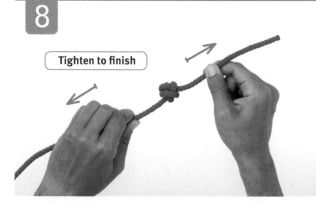

Stevedore Knot

- Good for preventing a line from slipping.
- Starts like the Figure of Eight (*see pp.38–39*), but its extra turn forms a bulkier knot that is less prone to jamming and easier to untie.
- Preferred by stevedores or dockworkers.

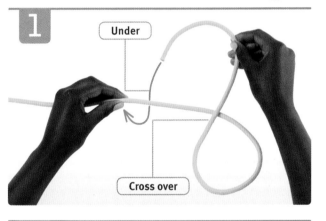

1

Under

Cross over

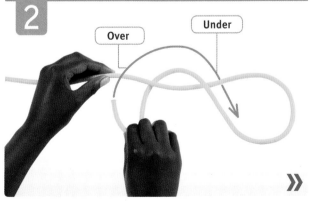

2

Over

Under

»

3

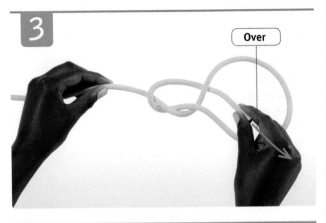

Over

4

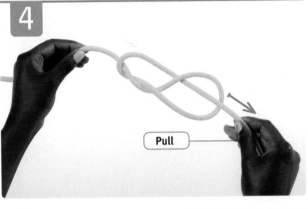

Pull

5

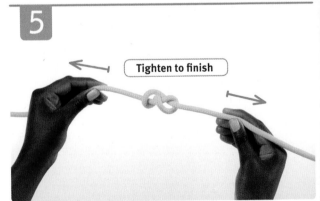

Tighten to finish

Monkey's Fist

- Adds extra weight to the end of a line that needs to be thrown.
- When working the knot into shape, ensure that all turns are even.
- When being used for decorative purposes, such as a key fob, place a wooden ball in the centre to add weight.

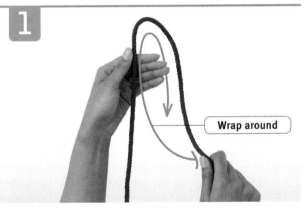

Wrap around

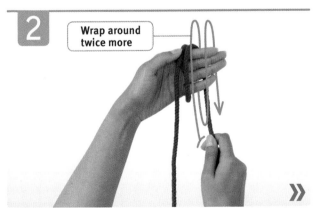

Wrap around twice more

»

3

Grip the bottom of the loops

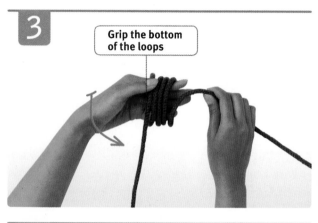

4

Wrap around

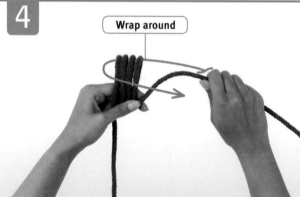

5

Wrap around three times

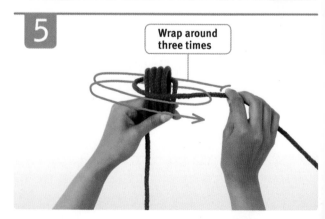

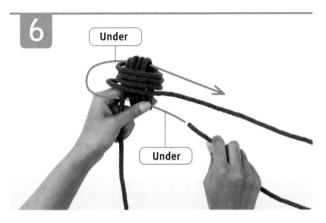

6

Under

Under

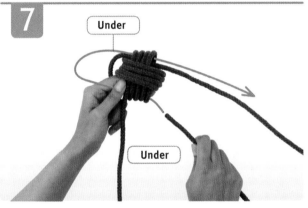

7

Under

Under

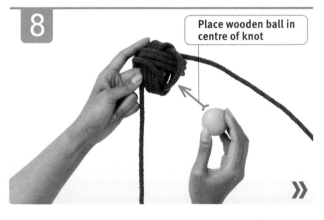

8

Place wooden ball in centre of knot

》

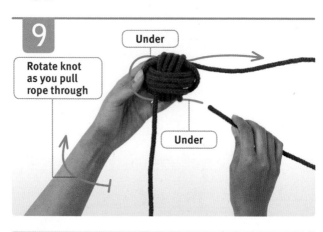

9

Rotate knot as you pull rope through

Under

Under

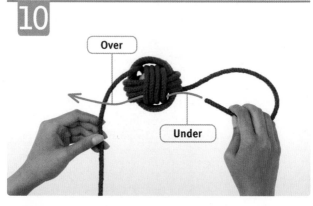

10

Over

Under

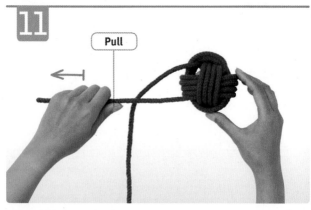

11

Pull

12

Work out slack

Push

Pull

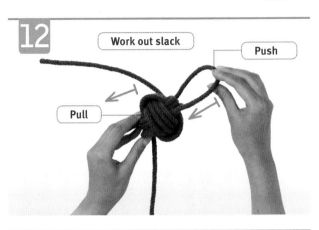

13

Work into shape

Pull

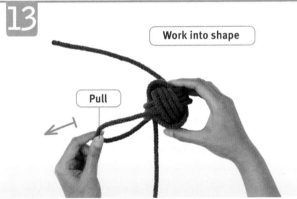

14

Trim and tuck
to finish

Crown Knot

- Used to prevent the ends of a three-strand rope from unravelling.
- Forms the basis of other decorative stoppers such as the Manrope Knot (*see pp.61–71*).
- Ensure that strand ends point downwards.

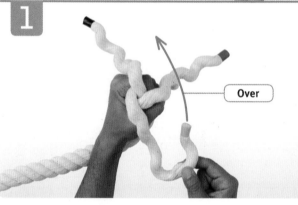

1

Over

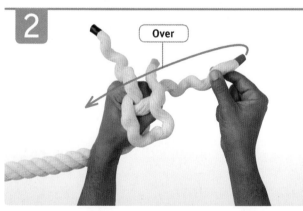

2

Over

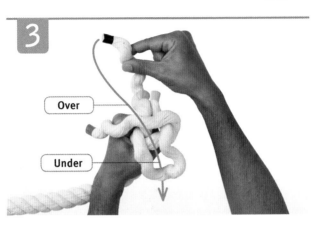

Over

Under

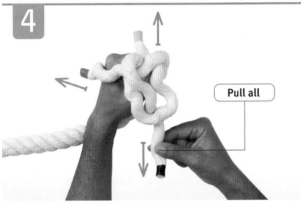

Pull all

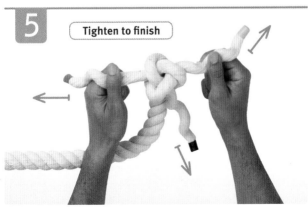

Tighten to finish

Wall Knot

- Used in combination with the Crown Knot (*see pp.54–55*) to make other decorative stopper knots such as the Manrope Knot (*see pp.61–71*).
- Whip (*see pp.374–75*) the ends before using as a stopper knot.
- Ensure the ends point upwards from the knot.
- Forms the basis of the Matthew Walker Knot (*see pp.58–60*).

1 UNLAY STRANDS AT THE END OF A ROPE (»p.21)

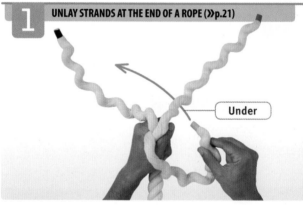

Under

2

Under

3

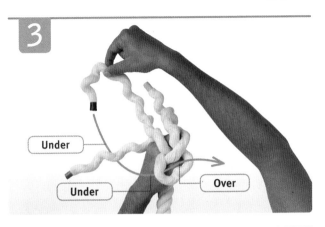

Under

Under | Over

4

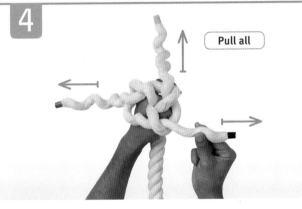

Pull all

5

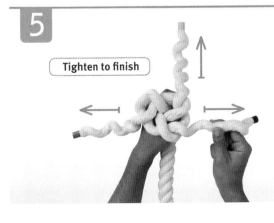

Tighten to finish

Matthew Walker Knot

- A stopper knot for three-strand rope.
- Can also be made with four strands.
- Traditionally tied at the end of a rope used as a handle for a wooden bucket.

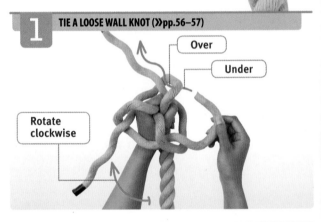

1 TIE A LOOSE WALL KNOT (»pp.56–57)

Over

Under

Rotate clockwise

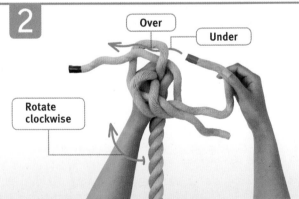

2

Over

Under

Rotate clockwise

3

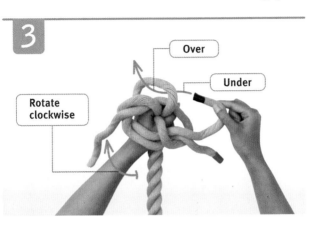

Over

Under

Rotate clockwise

4

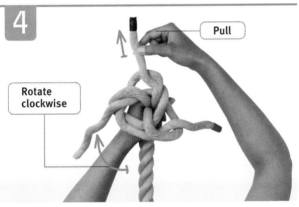

Pull

Rotate clockwise

5

Make a second cycle of tucks

》》

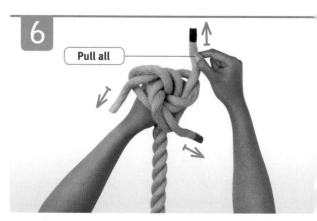

Pull all

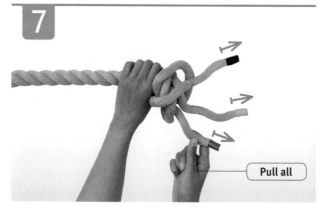

Pull all

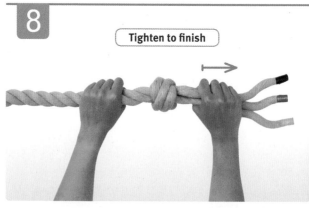

Tighten to finish

Manrope Knot

- A decorative stopper knot made by tying a Crown Knot (*see pp.54–55*) on top of a Wall Knot (*see pp.56–57*).
- Traditionally tied on the ends of handrail ropes used when boarding ships.
- Can be doubled but care must be taken that each strand is positioned on the same side as the previous one.

1 — TIE A WALL KNOT (»pp.56–57)

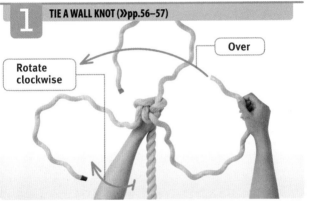

Over

Rotate clockwise

2

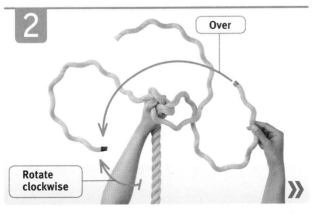

Over

Rotate clockwise

»

3

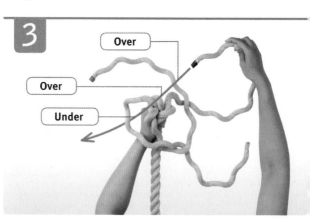

Over

Over

Under

4

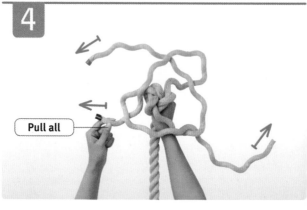

Pull all

5

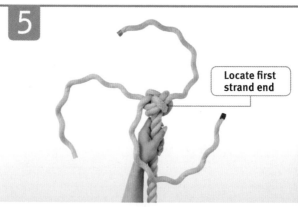

Locate first
strand end

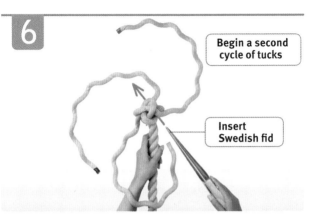

6

Begin a second cycle of tucks

Insert Swedish fid

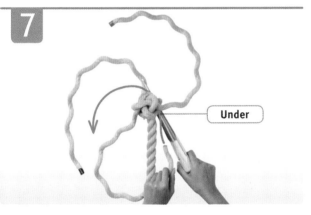

7

Under

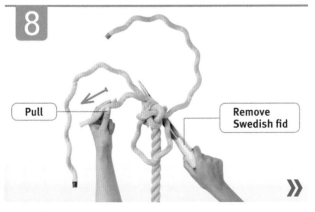

8

Pull

Remove Swedish fid

»

9

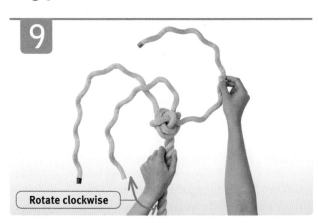

Rotate clockwise

10

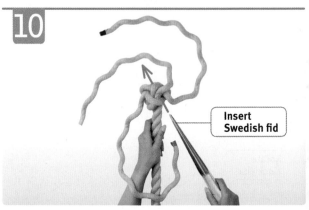

Insert Swedish fid

11

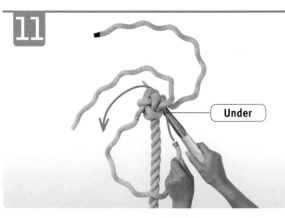

Under

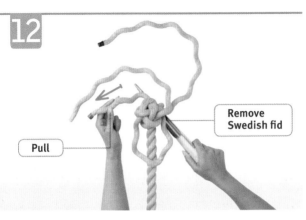

12

Pull

Remove Swedish fid

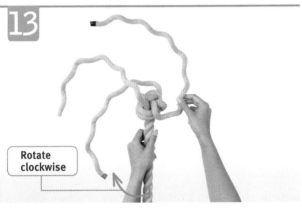

13

Rotate clockwise

14

Insert Swedish fid

»

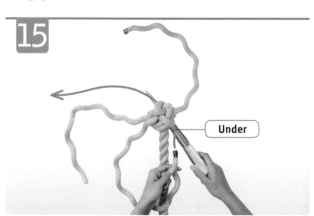

Under

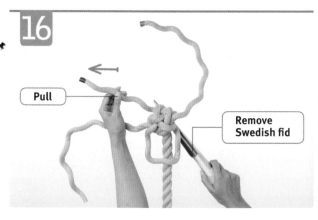

Pull

Remove
Swedish fid

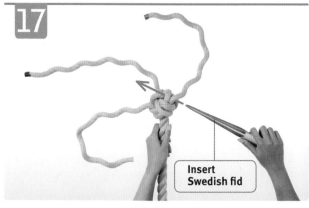

Insert
Swedish fid

18

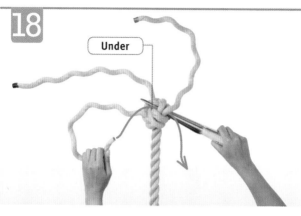

Under

19

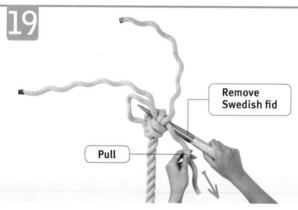

Remove
Swedish fid

Pull

20

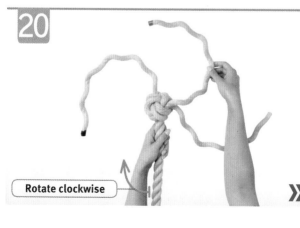

Rotate clockwise

»

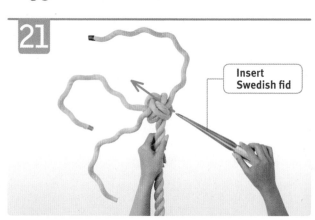

21

Insert
Swedish fid

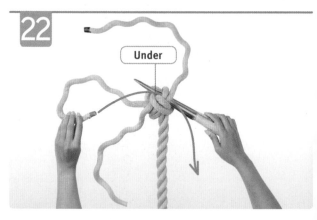

22

Under

23

Remove
Swedish fid

Pull

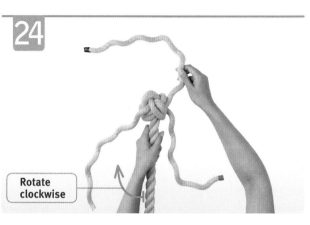

24

Rotate clockwise

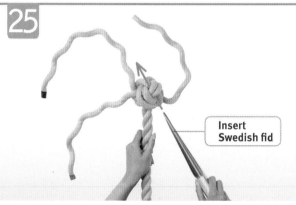

25

Insert Swedish fid

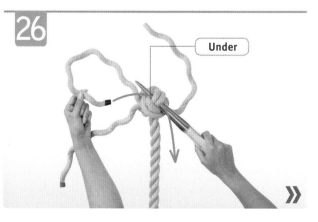

26

Under

»

27

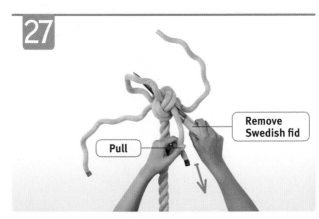

Remove
Swedish fid

Pull

28

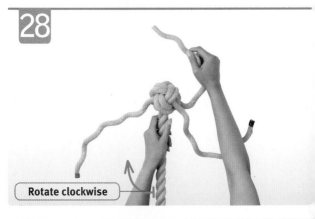

Rotate clockwise

29

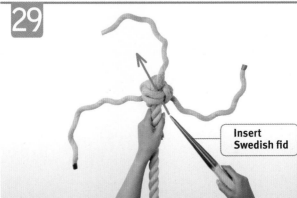

Insert
Swedish fid

30

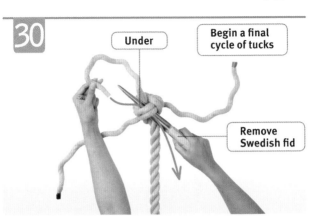

Under

Begin a final cycle of tucks

Remove Swedish fid

31

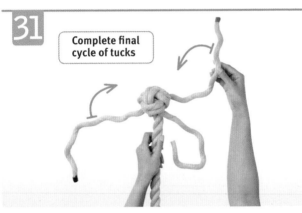

Complete final cycle of tucks

32

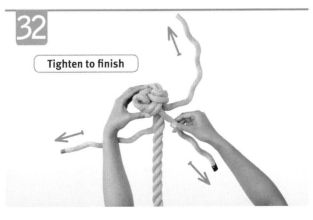

Tighten to finish

Diamond Knot

- A firm stopper knot tied in the strands of the rope.
- Made by tying a Wall Knot (*see pp.56–57*) below a Crown Knot (*see pp.54–55*).
- Sometimes used as an alternative to the Matthew Walker Knot (*see pp.58–60*).
- To make it easier to thread the strands, use a fid or Swedish fid (*see p.19*).

1 TIE A CROWN KNOT (»pp.54–55)

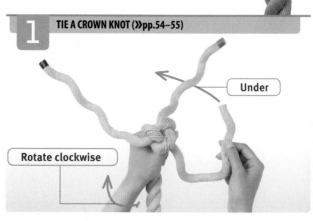

Under

Rotate clockwise

2

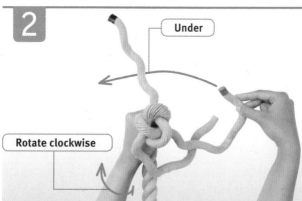

Under

Rotate clockwise

3

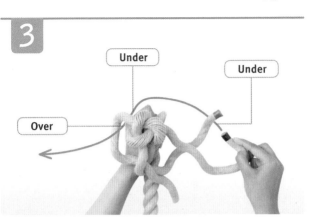

Over

Under

Under

4

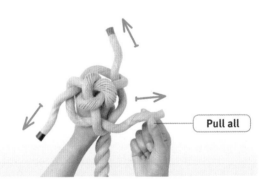

Pull all

5

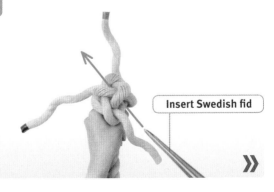

Insert Swedish fid

»

6

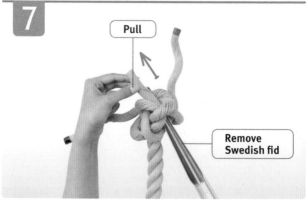

Under

7

Pull

Remove
Swedish fid

8

Arrange strands

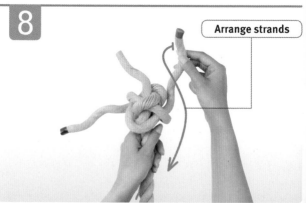

9

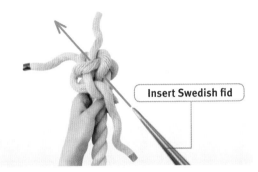

Insert Swedish fid

10

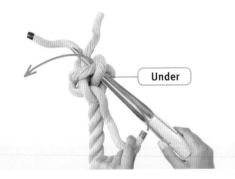

Under

11

Pull

Remove Swedish fid

»

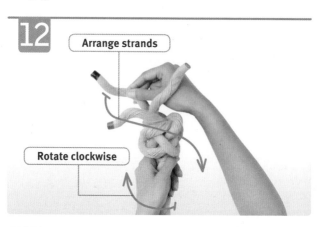

12

Arrange strands

Rotate clockwise

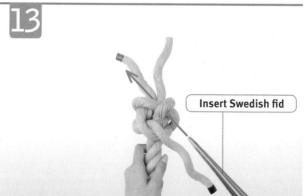

13

Insert Swedish fid

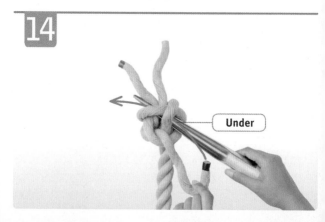

14

Under

15

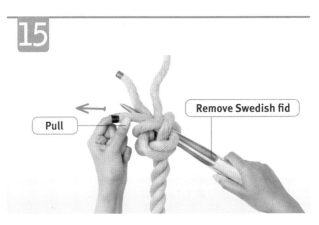

Pull

Remove Swedish fid

16

Pull all

17

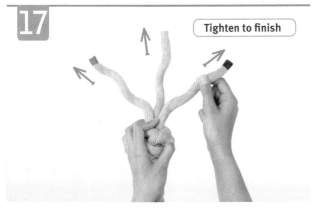

Tighten to finish

Binding Knots

Binding knots can be used to gather in sails, or to bind together a number of loose items such as timbers. They can also be used to tie a rope neatly around an object – for example, to wrap a gift.

True Lover's Knot

- A knot that symbolizes two people joined in love, sometimes found on a ring.
- Links two pieces of rope using interlocking Overhand Knots (*see pp.28–29*).
- The Overhand Knots should mirror each other perfectly.

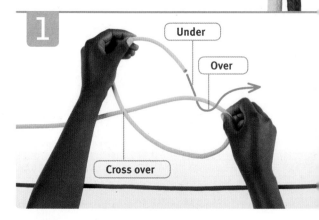

1

Under

Over

Cross over

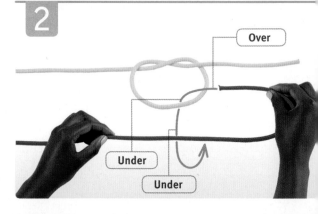

2

Over

Under

Under

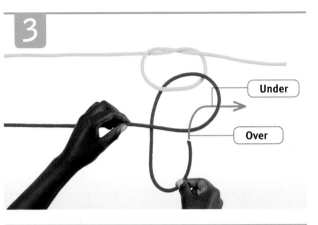

3

Under

Over

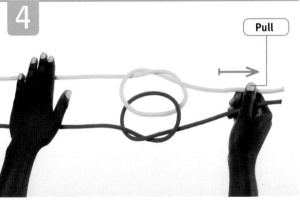

4

Pull

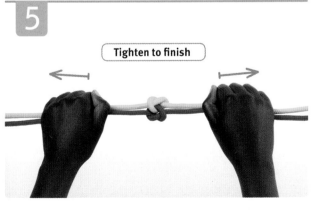

5

Tighten to finish

Sailor's Cross

- A decorative knot that symbolizes good luck.
- Developed from the True Lover's Knot (*see pp.80–81*).

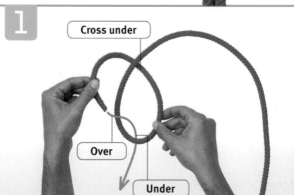

1

Cross under

Over

Under

2

Over

Under

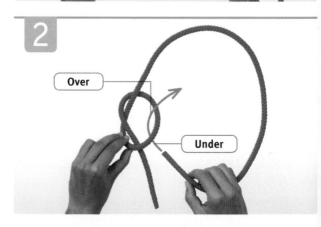

3

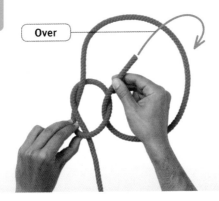

Over

4

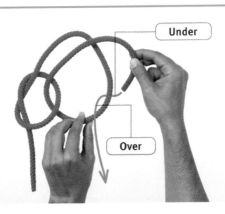

Under

Over

5

Reach through and grip

Reach through and grip

6

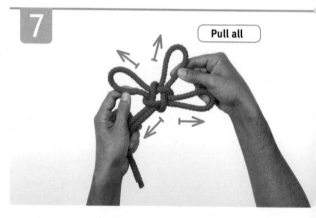

Pull   Pull

7

Pull all

8

Straighten to finish

Reef Knot

- A simple binding knot for securing a rope around an object.
- Derives its name from being tied around a bundle of sail.
- Also known as the Square Knot.

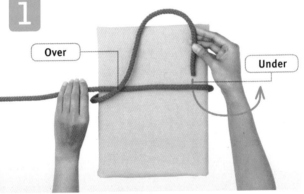

1

Over

Under

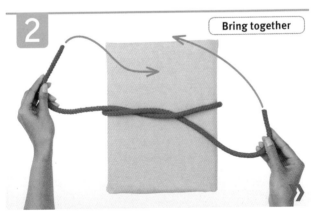

2

Bring together

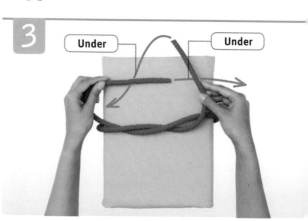

3

Under   Under

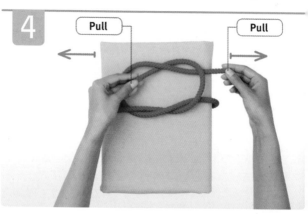

4

Pull   Pull

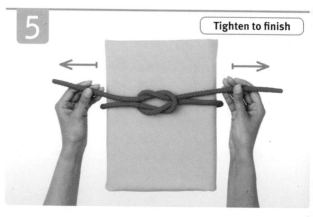

5

Tighten to finish

Slipped Reef Knot

- A quick-release version of the Reef Knot (*see pp.85–86*).
- Start with a long working end to ensure there is enough rope to form a bight.
- Can be undone by tugging on the short end of the bight.

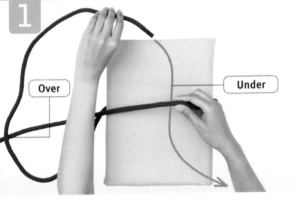

1

Over   Under

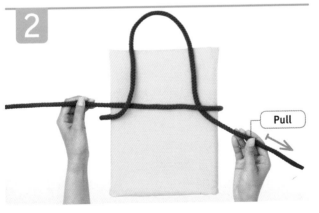

2

Pull

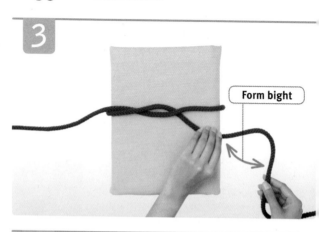

3

Form bight

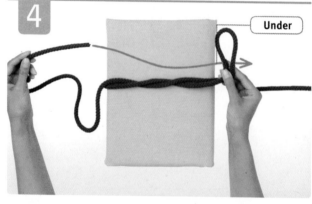

4

Under

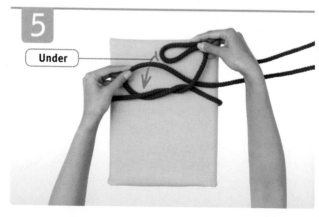

5

Under

6

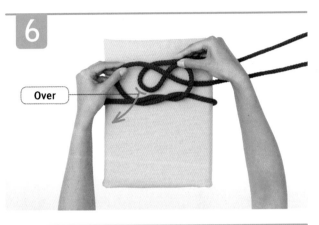

Over

7

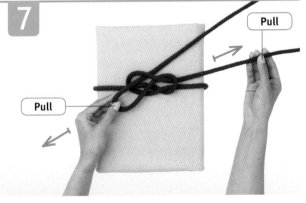

Pull

Pull

8

Tighten to finish

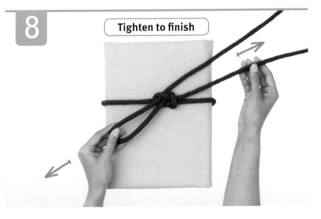

Slipped Reef Knot Doubled

- Commonly used for tying shoelaces.
- Can also be tied with ribbon to make a bow around a package.
- Formed with two bights.

1

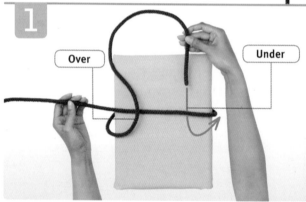

Over

Under

2

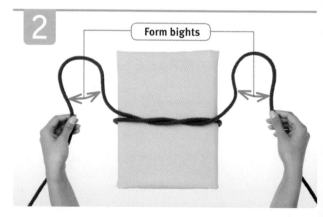

Form bights

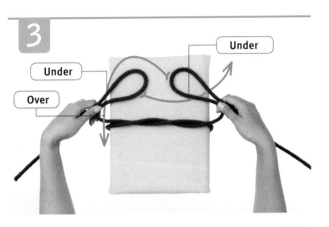

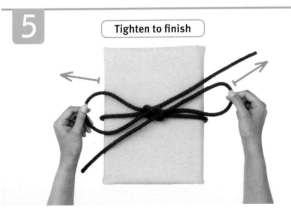

Granny Knot

- An incorrectly formed version of the Reef Knot (*see pp.85–86*) – does not have the same square form.
- Not as stable as the Reef Knot – may slip or jam.

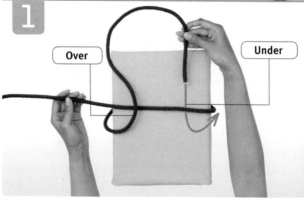

Over

Under

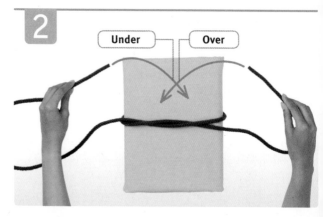

Under

Over

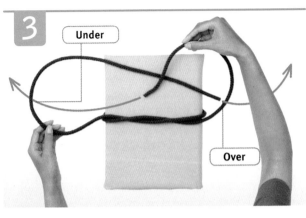

3

Under

Over

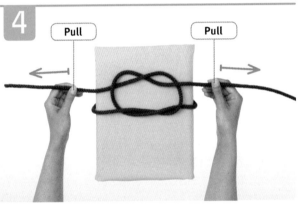

4

Pull

Pull

5

Tighten to finish

Thief Knot

- An unusual binding knot used to secure a rope or line around an object.
- Easily confused with, although much less secure than, the Reef Knot (see pp.85–86).
- Historically used by sailors to safeguard their bags – a thief would be likely to simply retie the bag using a Reef Knot and thus betray their presence.

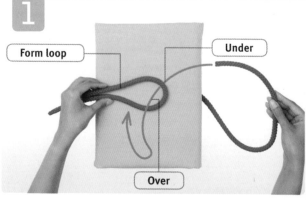

1

Form loop

Under

Over

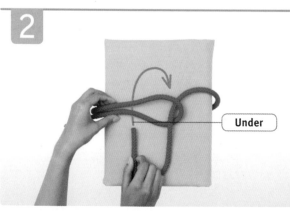

2

Under

3

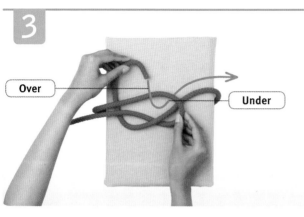

Over

Under

4

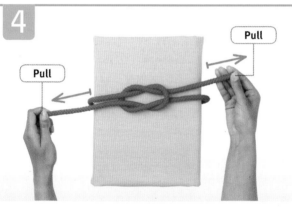

Pull

Pull

5

Tighten to finish

Surgeon's Knot

- A binding knot used by surgeons to tie sutures.
- Can also be tied around a bundle.
- If working with a bundle, draw it together by tightening the first two tucks before finishing the knot.
- The extra tuck holds the knot tight while the process is completed.

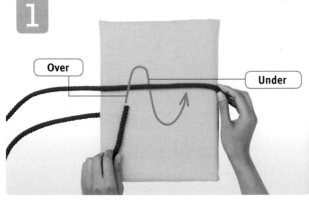

Over
Under

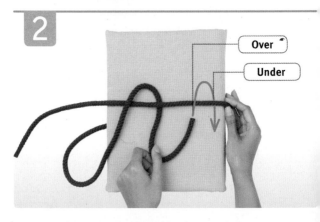

Over
Under

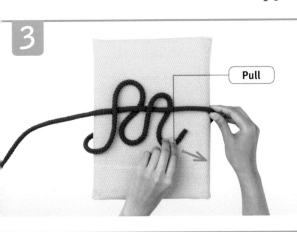

3 Pull

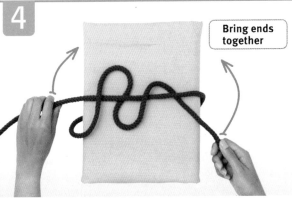

4 Bring ends together

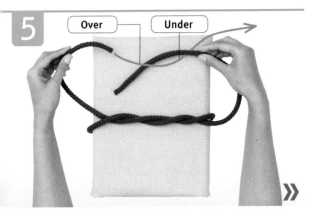

5 Over Under

»

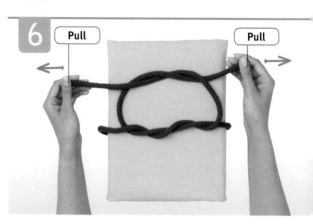

6 | Pull   Pull

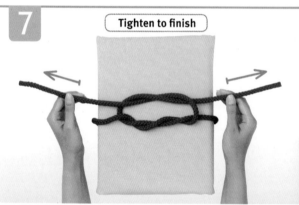

7 | Tighten to finish

Surgeon's Knot with Second Tuck

- A surgeon's knot made with an extra tuck.
- Useful when working with slippery rope.
- Tuck the right working end twice around the left working end at Step 5 (*see p.97*).

Turquoise Turtle

- The perfect knot for tying shoelaces.
- Rarely comes undone.
- Contains elements of the Reef Knot (*see pp.85–86*) and the Surgeon's Knot (*see pp.96–98*).
- To undo, pull the short ends.

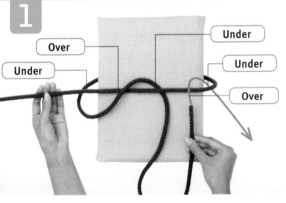

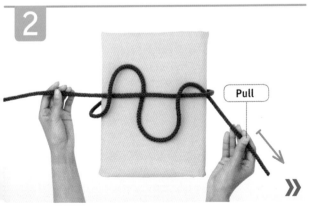

»

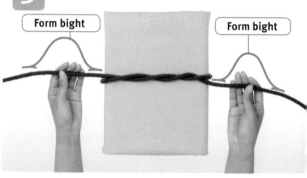

3

Form bight | Form bight

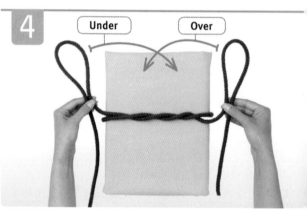

4

Under | Over

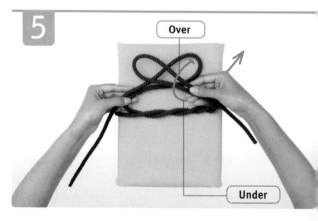

5

Over

Under

6

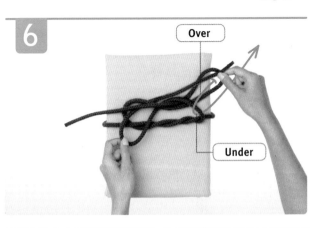

Over

Under

7

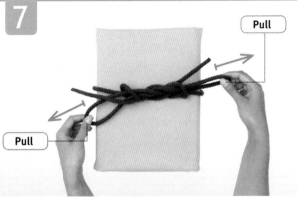

Pull

Pull

8

Tighten to finish

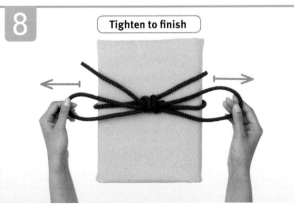

Packer's Knot

- Used to tie up a parcel or draw together a loose bundle or package.
- Based on the Figure of Eight (see pp.38–39).
- Secure with a half hitch (see p.23).

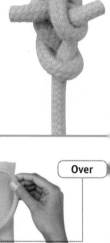

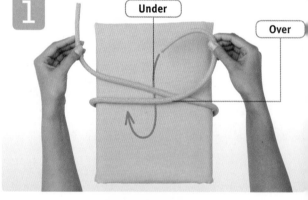

1

Under

Over

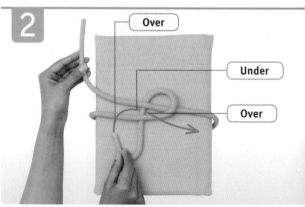

2

Over

Under

Over

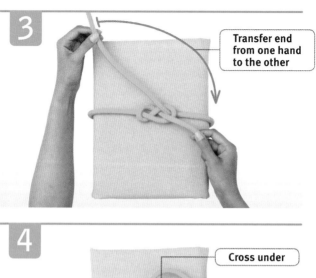

3

Transfer end
from one hand
to the other

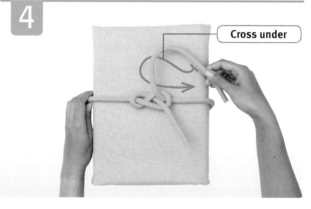

4

Cross under

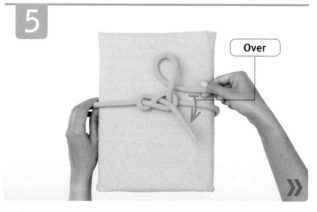

5

Over

6

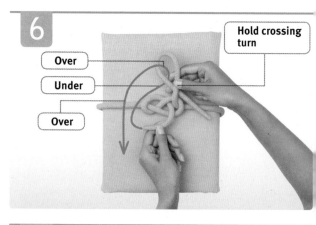

Over

Under

Over

Hold crossing turn

7

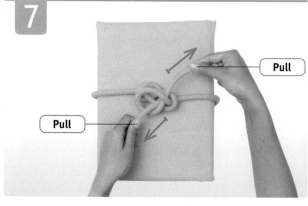

Pull

Pull

8

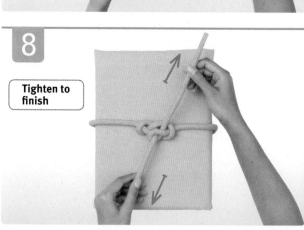

Tighten to finish

Clove Hitch

- A common, simple binding knot used when only one end of a rope is available to work with.
- Made from two half hitches (*see p.23*), both passed in the same direction.
- Used in most lashings (*see pp.211–24*).

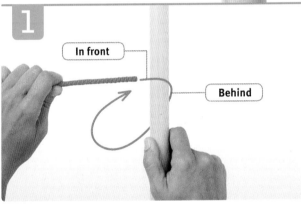

1

In front

Behind

2

In front

Behind

Over

»

3

In front

Under

4

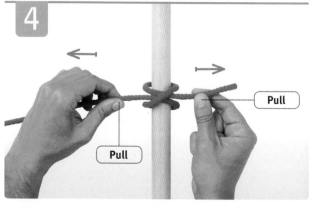

Pull

Pull

5

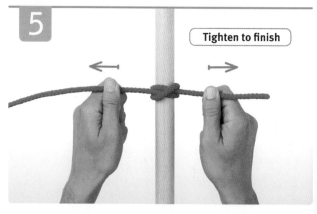

Tighten to finish

Clove Hitch – Second Method

- A common binding knot that is quick to tie.
- Can be tied in the middle of the rope.
- Made from two half hitches (*see p.23*), both passed in the same direction.
- Not completely secure – may work loose under strain.

1

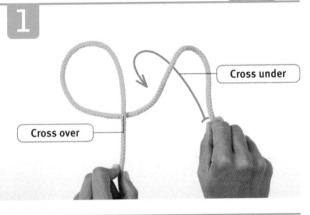

Cross under

Cross over

2

Place under · Place over

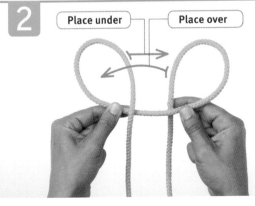

3

Arrange to form hole in centre

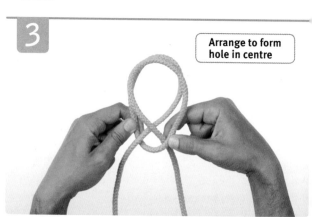

4

Lower onto pole

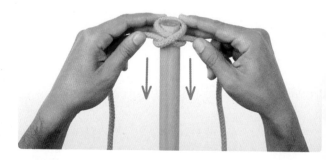

5

Tighten to finish

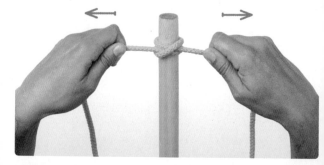

Constrictor Knot

- Makes a good temporary whipping (*see p.14*) or seizing (*see p.25*).
- Simple to tie but difficult to untie.
- Works best when tied in thin line.

1

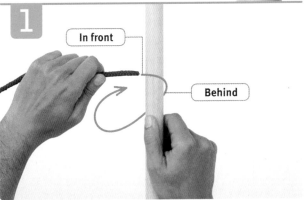

In front

Behind

2

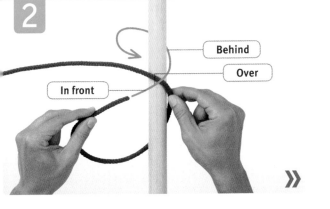

Behind

Over

In front

»

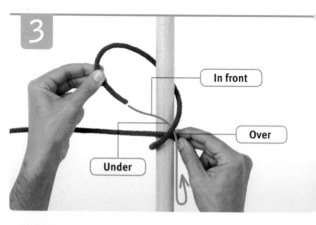

3

In front

Over

Under

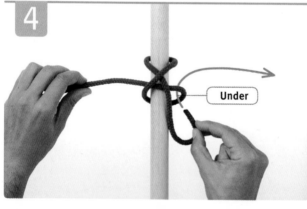

4

Under

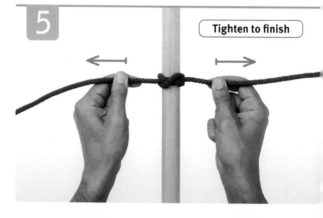

5

Tighten to finish

Timber Hitch

- Tied around a log or a bundle of timber.
- The harder the final pull, the tighter and more secure the knot becomes.
- The starting point for a Diagonal Lashing (*see pp.215–17*).

1

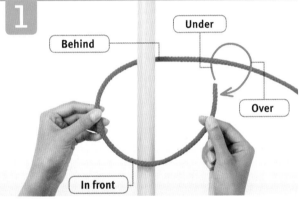

Behind · Under · Over · In front

2

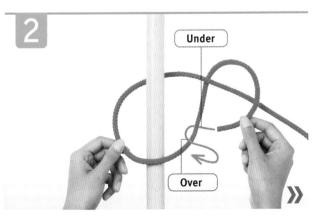

Under · Over

»

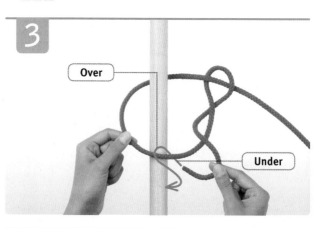

3

Over

Under

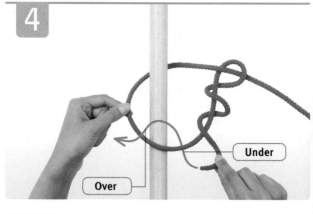

4

Under

Over

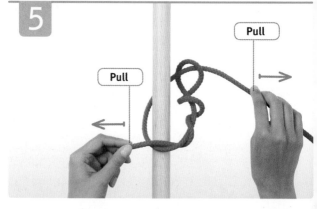

5

Pull

Pull

6

Pull

Pull

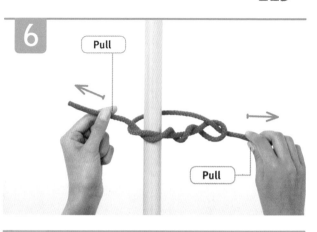

7

Tighten to finish

Pulling a Pole

- An extra half hitch (*see p.23*) can be added to the pole if it is to be dragged through water or across land.

- The half hitch prevents the pole from swaying around when it is moved.

Finish with half hitch

Boa Knot

- Used to secure or tie together cylindrical objects where a decorative as well as a practical knot is required.
- Should only be used when it can be slipped over the end of the object to which it is to be tied.
- Can be used instead of the Constrictor Knot (*see pp.109–10*).

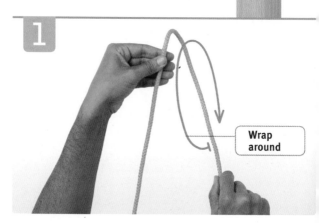

1

Wrap around

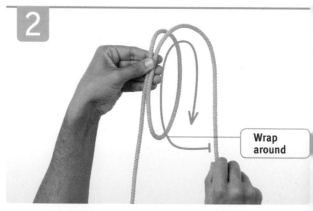

2

Wrap around

3

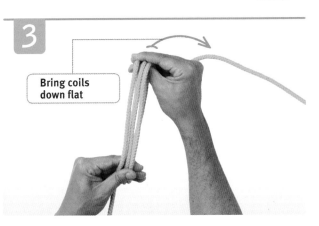

Bring coils down flat

4

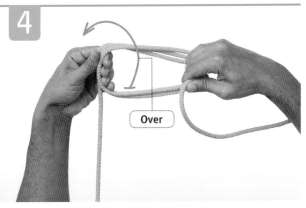

Over

5

Fold over

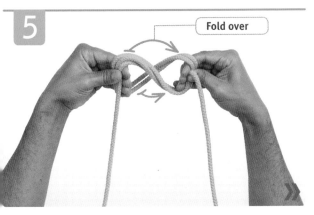

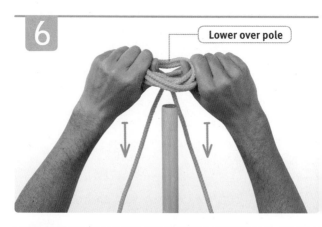

6   Lower over pole

7   Work into shape

8   Tighten to finish

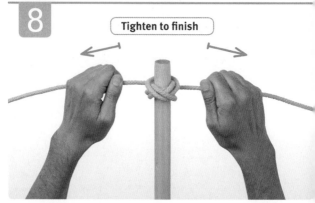

Turk's Head – Three-Lead Four-Bight

- A decorative knot usually tied around a pole or rail.
- Can also be flattened out into a mat.
- Can be doubled or tripled (*see p.24*).

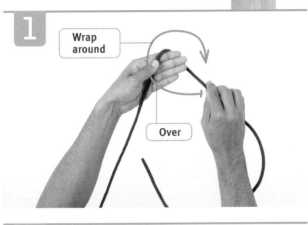

1

Wrap around

Over

2

Over

Under

Under

»

3

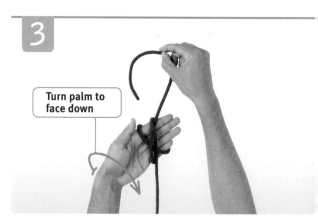

Turn palm to face down

4

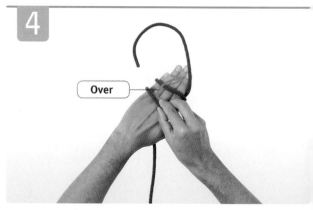

Over

5

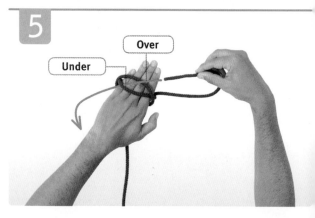

Over

Under

6

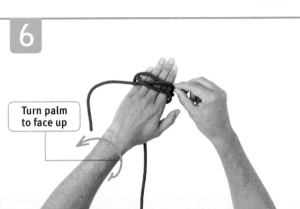

Turn palm to face up

7

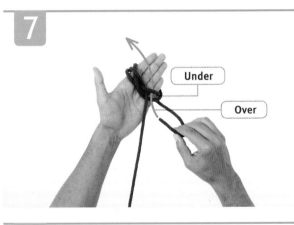

Under

Over

8

Turn palm to face down

»

9

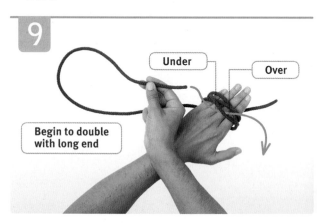

Under

Over

Begin to double
with long end

10

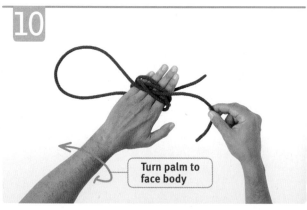

Turn palm to
face body

11

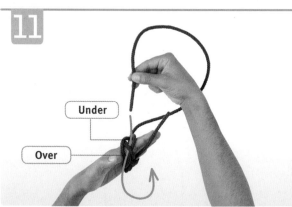

Under

Over

12

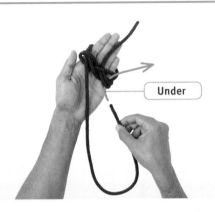

Under

13

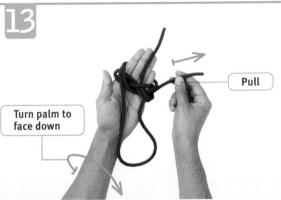

Turn palm to face down

Pull

14

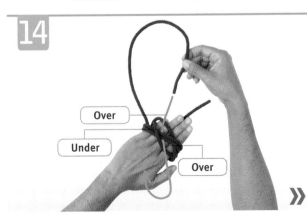

Over

Under

Over

»

15

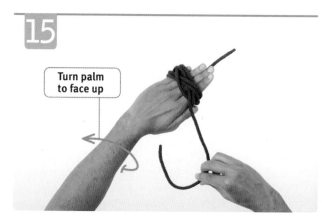

Turn palm to face up

16

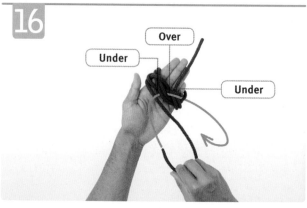

Under

Over

Under

17

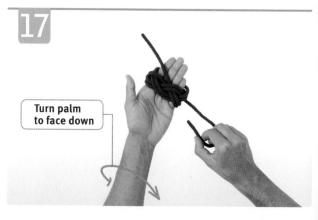

Turn palm to face down

18

Over | Under

19

Turn palm to face up

20

Trim and tuck to finish

BEST FOR ...
Household

Everyday knots can be used around the home for all kinds of tasks – from hanging pictures and tying back curtains to securing a washing line, making decorative bows, and tying shoelaces.

Round Turn and Two Half Hitches » pp.180–81

✅ Ideal for attaching picture cord to the hanging rings or screw eyes on the back of picture frames.

✅ Also useful for tying a line to a fixed object, such as a washing line to its pole.

✅ Can be untied even when under strain.

Similar knots:
» pp.182–83
Buntline Hitch
» pp.184–85
Fisherman's Bend

Manrope Knot » pp.61–71

✅ A perfect knot for tying back curtains when threaded through an Eye Splice (*see pp.342–46*).

✅ Can also make an end for a rope handrail.

✅ Can be made bulkier by following the pattern around for a third time.

Similar knots:
» pp.49–53
Monkey's Fist
» pp.72–77
Diamond Knot

Turquoise Turtle
» pp.99–101

✓ A two-loop knot that is quick to tie.

✓ Perfect for tying up the laces on shoes or boots as it rarely comes undone.

✓ Can be used to make a secure yet decorative bow on a parcel or a present.

Similar knots:
» pp.87–89
Slipped Reef Knot

Constrictor Knot
» pp.109–10

✓ A perfect replacement for a hose clip.

✓ Can also be used with stiff cord to tie up the neck of a bin bag or sack.

✓ Binds tightly, making it very hard to untie.

Similar knots:
» pp.107–08
Clove Hitch – Second Method
» pp.114–16
Boa Knot

Packer's Knot » pp.102–04

✓ A binding knot that is perfect for tying up a parcel, as it is easy to pull tight and lock into position.

✓ The knot's tightening feature is good for baling up bundles of newspaper.

✓ Also known as a Butcher's Knot, as it can be used to prepare joints of meat for roasting.

Similar knots:
» pp.87–89
Slipped Reef Knot
» pp.96–98
Surgeon's Knot

Waggoner's Hitch
» pp.203–04

✓ Pefect for tying down a load such as a pile of logs. It will undo as soon as the strain is released.

✓ Will also secure a roof box to the top of a car.

✗ If repeatedly tied in the same place this knot can cause the rope to chafe severely.

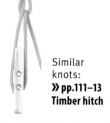

Similar knots:
» pp.111–13
Timber hitch

Turk's Head – Four-Lead Five-Bight

- Used mainly for decorative purposes.
- Essentially a continuous Four-Strand Flat Plait (*see pp.294–95*) – can be followed around two, three, or four times.
- Adjust the spaces between the strands as you tie to ensure that they are even.

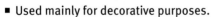

1

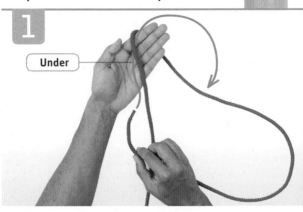

Under

2

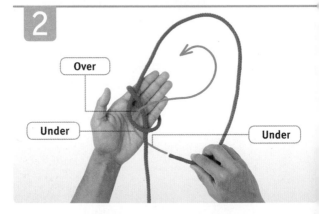

Over

Under

Under

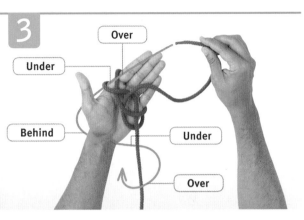

3

Over

Under

Behind

Under

Over

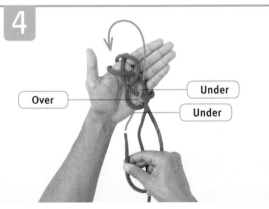

4

Over

Under

Under

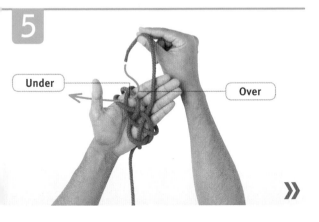

5

Under

Over

»

6

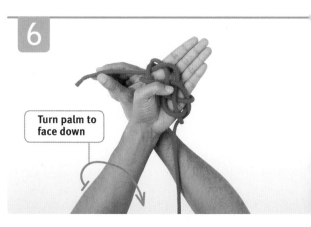

Turn palm to face down

7

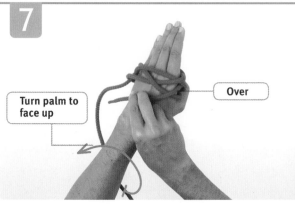

Turn palm to face up

Over

8

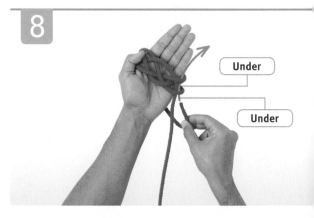

Under

Under

9

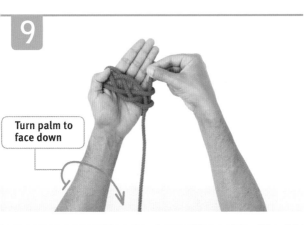

Turn palm to face down

10

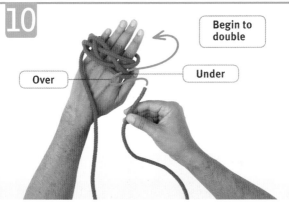

Begin to double

Over

Under

11

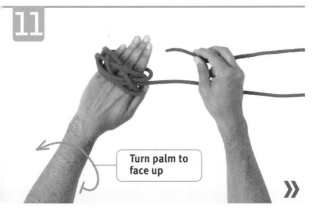

Turn palm to face up

»

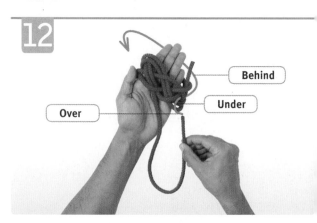

12

Behind

Over

Under

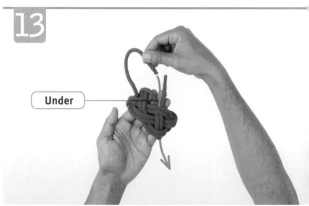

13

Under

14

Trim and tuck
to finish

Turk's Head – Five-Lead Four-Bight

- A highly decorative knot with a large number of interwoven strands.
- Can be doubled or tripled (*see p.24*).
- Finish by tightening carefully then trimming and tucking the ends inside the knot.

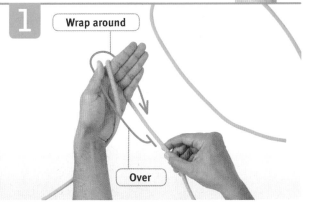

1 Wrap around / Over

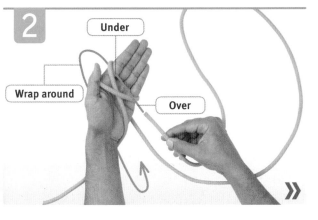

2 Under / Wrap around / Over

»

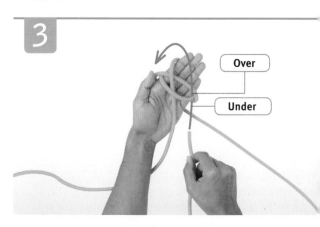

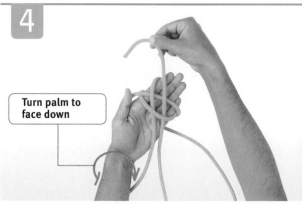

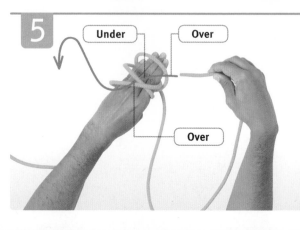

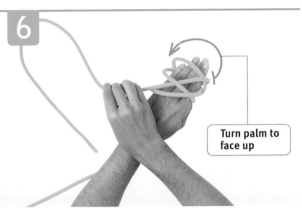

6

Turn palm to face up

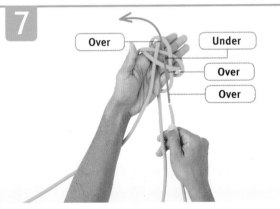

7

Over

Under

Over

Over

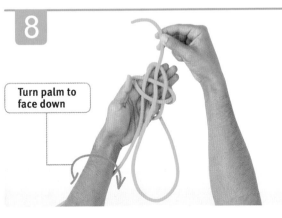

8

Turn palm to face down

»

9

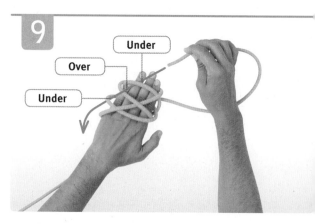

Under

Over

Under

10

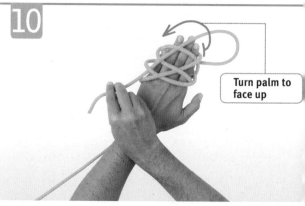

Turn palm to face up

11

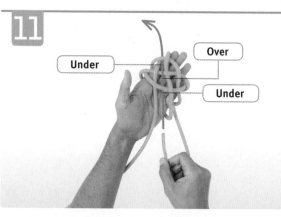

Under

Over

Under

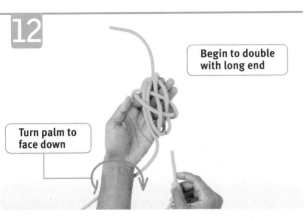

12

Begin to double with long end

Turn palm to face down

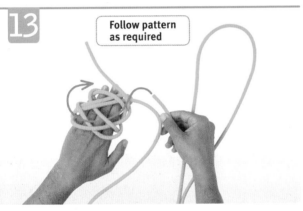

13

Follow pattern as required

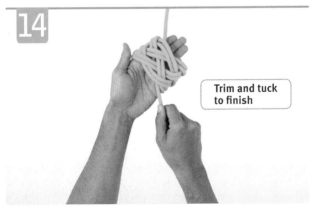

14

Trim and tuck to finish

Bends

A bend is used to connect two pieces of rope or line together. Most bends are designed to tie together two ropes of equal diameter, but there are also bends that have been developed for ropes of different thicknesses.

Sheet Bend

- A common knot for joining two ropes of equal thickness.
- Quick and easy to tie.
- May work loose when not under strain.
- If joining ropes of unequal size, use the Double Sheet Bend (*see pp.144–45*).

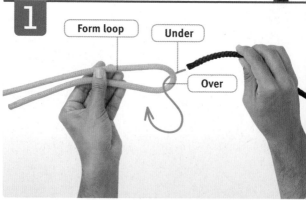

1

Form loop   Under

Over

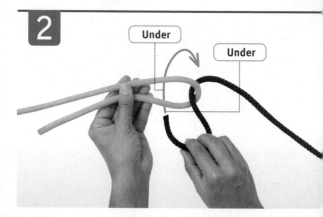

2

Under   Under

3

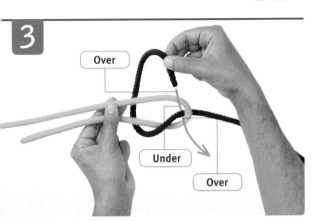

Over

Under

Over

4

Pull

5

Tighten to finish

Tucked Sheet Bend

- Used for joining two pieces of thin line.
- A variation of the Sheet Bend (*see pp.140–41*) that incorporates a Figure of Eight (*see pp.38–39*) structure.
- Tuck ends against rope to prevent snagging when pulled along.
- Will snag if pulled in the wrong direction.

1

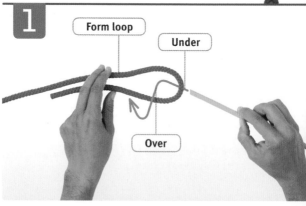

Form loop

Under

Over

2

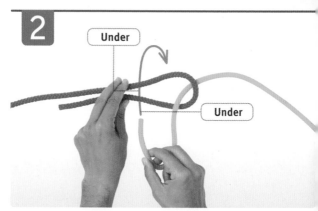

Under

Under

3

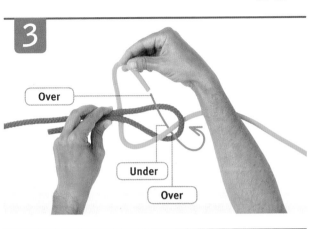

Over

Under

Over

4

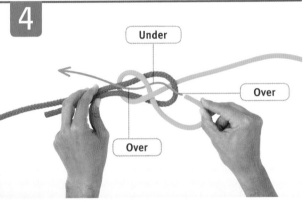

Under

Over

Over

5

Tighten to finish

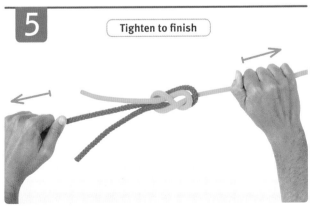

Double Sheet Bend

- Used to join two ropes of unequal thickness.
- Use the thicker rope to form the loop.

1

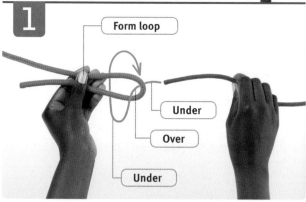

Form loop

Under

Over

Under

2

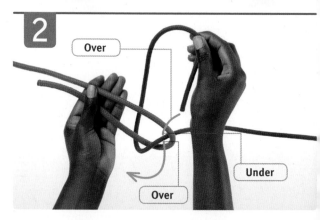

Over

Under

Over

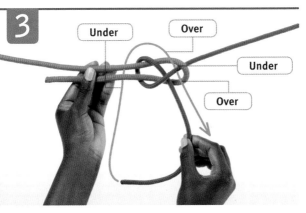

3

Under | Over

Under

Over

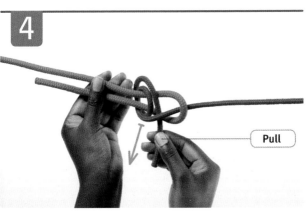

4

Pull

5

Tighten to finish

Rope Yarn Knot

- Used for tying together rope yarns to make a new piece of rope.
- Can also be used to join textile materials together.
- Similar in structure to the Reef Knot (*see pp.85–86*) but less bulky.

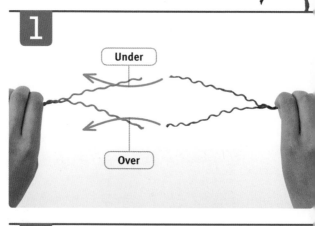

1

Under

Over

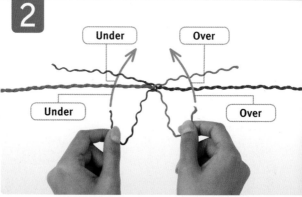

2

Under | Over

Under | Over

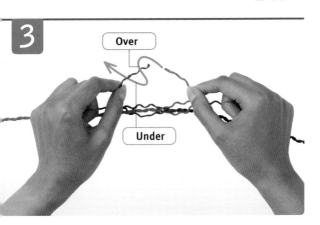

3

Over

Under

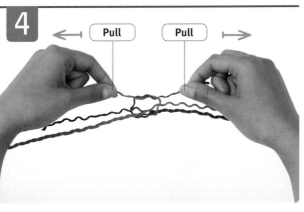

4

Pull   Pull

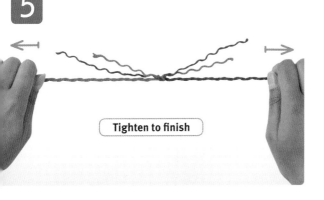

5

Tighten to finish

Carrick Bend

- Good for joining two thick ropes or cables.
- Can be seized (*see p.25*) as a flat knot, or tightened to collapse on itself.
- Easy to untie.

1

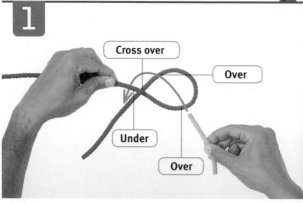

Cross over

Over

Under

Over

2

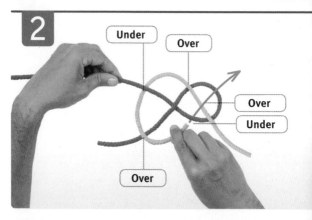

Under

Over

Over

Under

Over

3

Pull

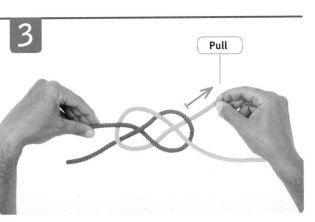

4

Pull

Short ends swap position as you pull

Pull

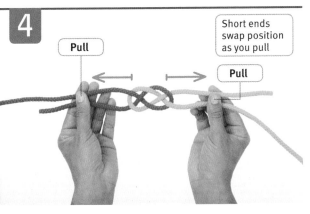

5

Tighten to finish

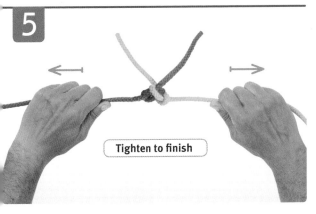

Hunter's Bend

- Good for joining two lengths of synthetic rope (*see also pp.140–41*).
- Needs to be carefully adjusted to shape.
- Also known as the Rigger's Bend.
- Named after Dr Edward Hunter.

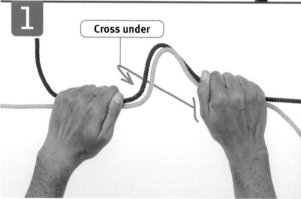

1

Cross under

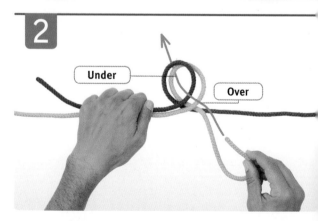

2

Under

Over

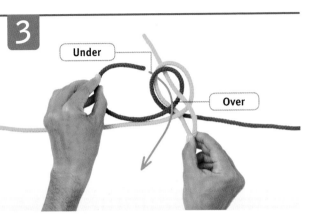

3

Under

Over

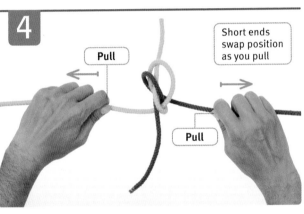

4

Pull

Short ends
swap position
as you pull

Pull

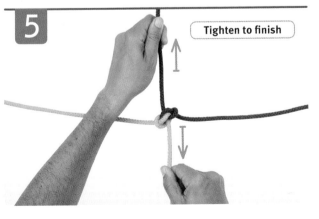

5

Tighten to finish

Lanyard Knot

- A decorative method for joining two ropes.
- Based on the same structure as the Carrick Bend (*see pp.148–49*).
- Also known as the Friendship Knot.

1

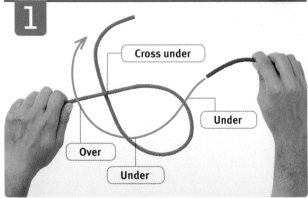

Cross under

Under

Over

Under

2

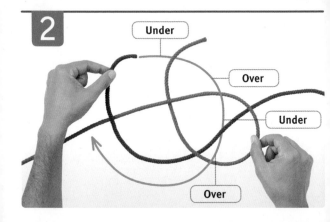

Under

Over

Under

Over

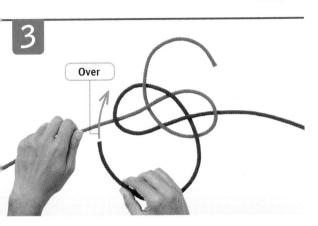

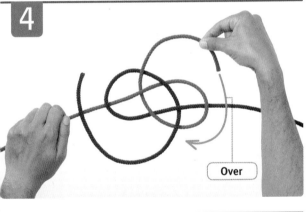

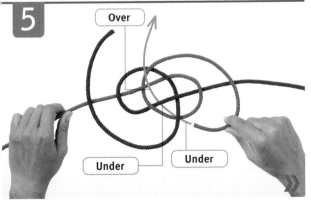

6

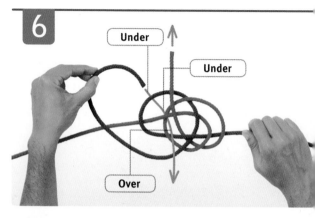

Under

Under

Over

7

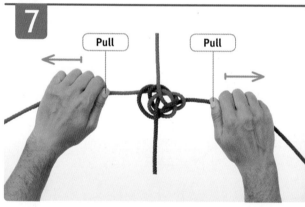

Pull

Pull

8

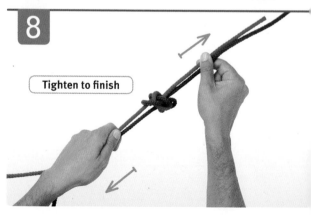

Tighten to finish

Ashley's Bend

- Used to join two pieces of thin line together.
- Easy to tie and untie.
- Secure even when subjected to strenuous movement.
- Ensure that both crossing turns are the same.
- Named after Clifford W. Ashley, an American knot expert.

1

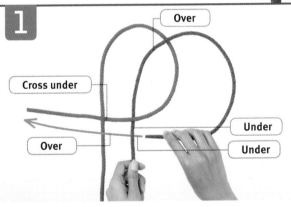

Over

Cross under

Over

Under

Under

2

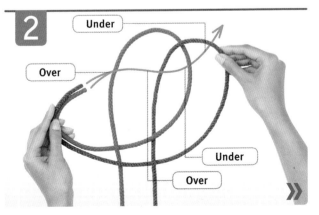

Under

Over

Under

Over

3

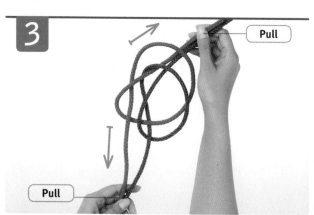

Pull

Pull

4

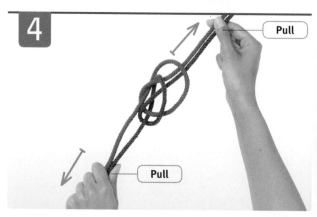

Pull

Pull

5

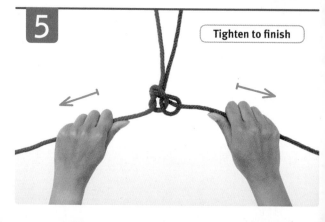

Tighten to finish

Fisherman's Knot

- Good for joining relatively thin ropes and lines.
- Used by fishermen and climbers.
- Ensure that the lengths of the short ends are at least five times the diameter of the rope.
- Consists of two sliding Overhand Knots (*see pp.28–29*).

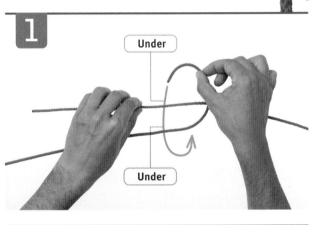

1

Under

Under

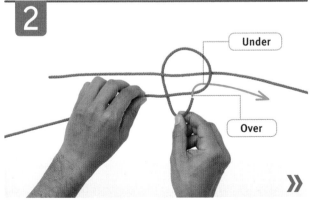

2

Under

Over

»

3

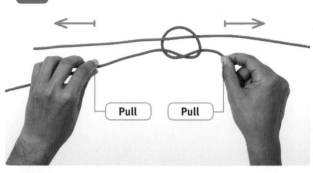

Pull

Pull

4

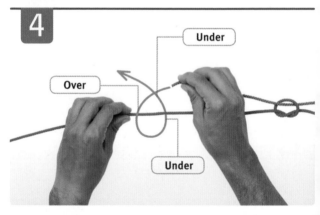

Under

Over

Under

5

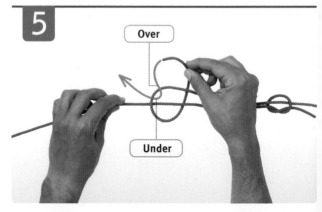

Over

Under

6

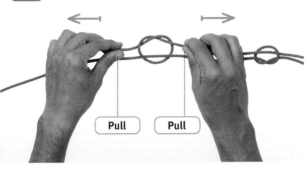

Pull   Pull

7

Bring knots together

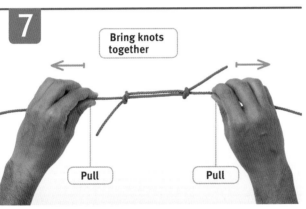

Pull   Pull

8

Tighten to finish

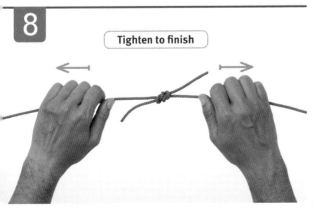

Double Fisherman's Knot

- Used when a rope or line is particularly slippery.
- The extra turns prevent the knot from coming undone when put under strain.
- The ends may be taped down for greater security.

1

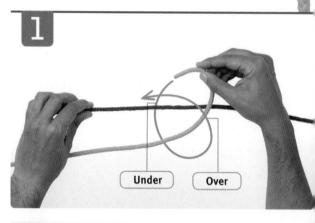

Under   Over

2

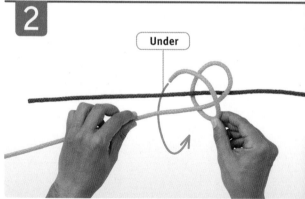

Under

3

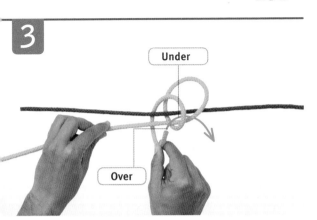

Under

Over

4

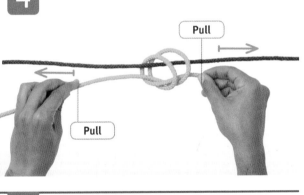

Pull

Pull

5

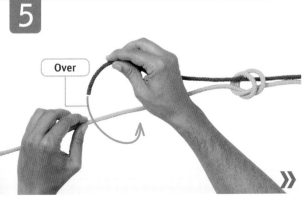

Over

》

6

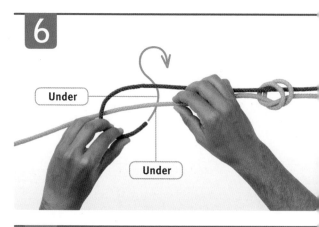

Under

Under

7

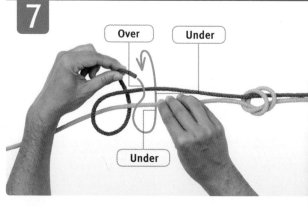

Over

Under

Under

8

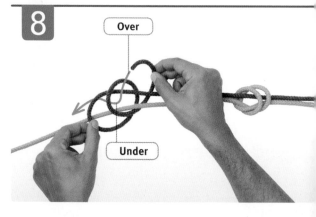

Over

Under

9

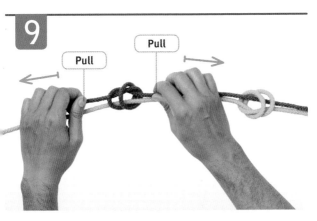

Pull

Pull

10

Bring knots together

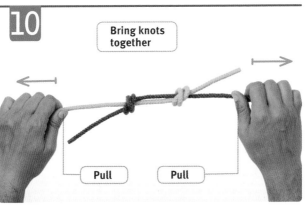

Pull

Pull

11

Tighten to finish

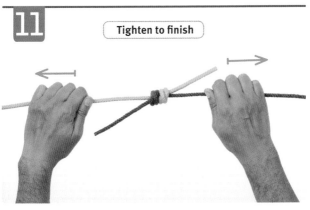

BEST FOR ...
Climbing

A knowledge of knots is essential for climbers, as their safety may depend on it. It is important to take care when finishing these common climbing knots – check the shape is correct and make sure there are no twists in the rope.

Italian Hitch
» pp.234–35

✓ Used on a safety line by climbers as it can control the speed of a fall and the distance fallen.

✓ A knot that can also be used for abseiling.

✗ Creates twists in the rope and causes wear, so best used as a backup or in an emergency.

Similar knots:
» p.235 Reversed Italian Hitch

Prusik Knot » pp.228–29

✓ Will slide when not under strain, so useful for providing handholds and footholds on ascent and descent.

✓ Extra turns can be added to give more friction if the rope is slippery or wet.

✗ Always check that the knot is secure and holds under strain.

Similar knots:
» pp.232–33 Klemheist Knot

Figure-of-Eight Loop
» pp.249–50

✅ Popular among climbers as its distinctive shape makes it easy to check that it has been tied properly.

✅ Still possesses some residual strength as an overhand loop, even if it is not tied properly.

Similar knots:
» pp.240–41
Bowline
» pp.253–54
Overhand Loop

Double Fisherman's Knot » pp.160–63

✅ Excellent for making continuous loops for Prusik slings (*see pp.228–29*).

✅ Also good for joining two lengths of rope, even if they are of different diameters.

✅ The chance of snagging can be reduced by taping the ends.

Similar knots:
» pp.157–59
Fisherman's Knot
» pp.172–73
Water Knot

Alpine Butterfly » pp.238–39

✓ Can be quickly tied in the middle of the rope without needing to have access to either of the rope ends.

✓ Ideal for attaching a middleman on a climb as strain can be applied to either side of the knot.

Similar knots:
» pp.249–50
Figure-of-Eight Loop
» pp.259–61
Bowline on the Bight

Bowline with Stopper
» p.248

✓ A variation on a Bowline which makes a good stopper at the end of a rope.

✓ Bulky and, when tight, easier to untie than a Figure of Eight or a Double Overhand Knot.

Similar knots:
» pp.242–44
Bowline – Second Method
» pp.245–47 **Bowline with Two Turns**

Blood Knot

- An effective method for joining together two pieces of thin line, such as fishing line.
- If tying with nylon, moisten the line to help draw it tight.
- Almost impossible to untie.
- Also known as the Barrel Knot.

1

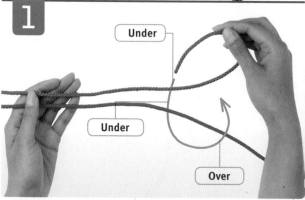

Under

Under

Over

2

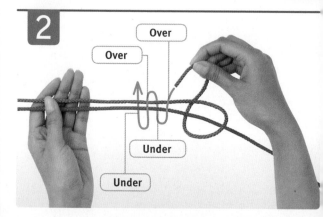

Over

Over

Under

Under

3

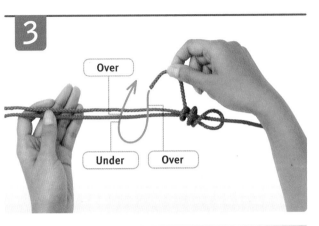

Over

Under   Over

4

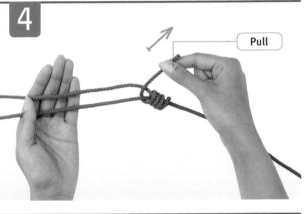

Pull

5

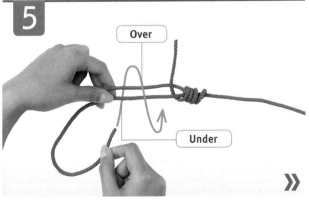

Over

Under

»

6

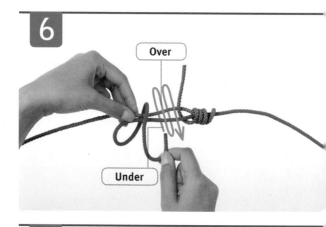

Over

Under

7

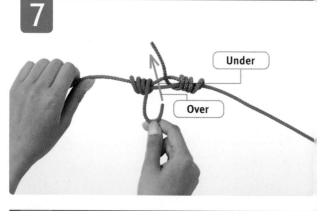

Under

Over

8

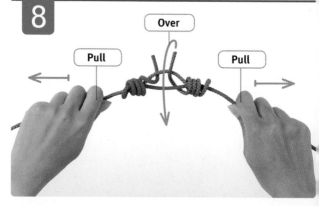

Over

Pull

Pull

9

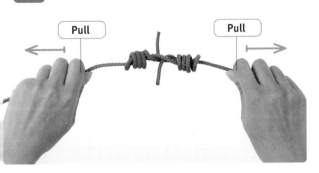

Pull

Pull

10

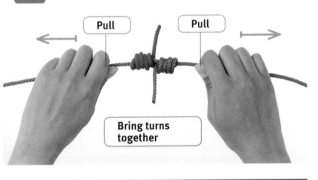

Pull

Pull

Bring turns together

11

Trim short ends to finish, if required

Water Knot

- Good for binding two ropes together.
- Will also work well with climber's flat tape.
- Work into a neat, flat arrangement.
- Based on the structure of the Overhand Knot (*see pp.28–29*).
- Also known as the Double Overhand Bend.

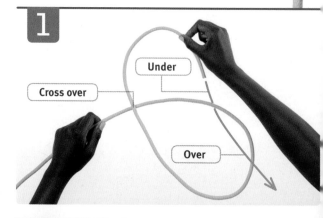

1

Cross over

Under

Over

2

Over

Under

Over

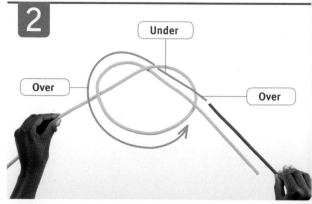

3

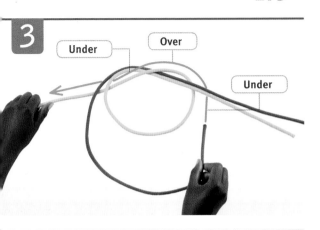

Under

Over

Under

4

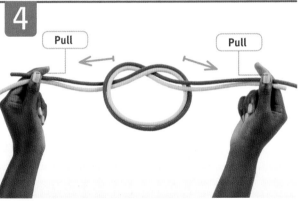

Pull

Pull

5

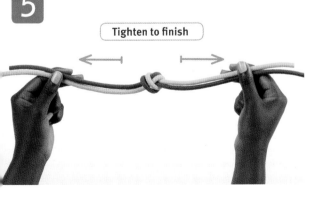

Tighten to finish

Hitches

A hitch is tied to secure a rope to an object, such as a pole or ring. Many hitches – especially those that are used by sailors – are designed to be both quick to tie and easy to undo.

Rolling Hitch

- Can be used to take strain off another rope or pole.
- Suitable for use when the pull on the rope is coming from a low angle, or from the side.
- Will only slide in one direction along the pole or rope.
- Will lock if pulled in the other direction.

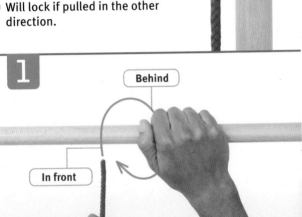

Behind

In front

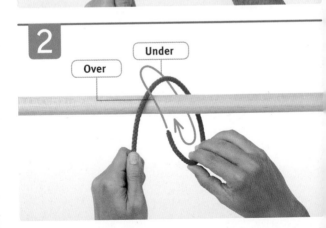

Over

Under

3

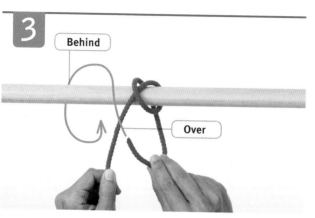

Behind

Over

4

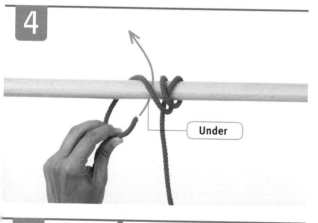

Under

5

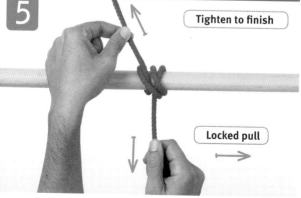

Tighten to finish

Locked pull

Mirrored Rolling Hitch

- Used to tie a rope to a pole or to take strain off another rope.
- Ensure that the second turn locks over the first.
- Make sure that the knot is tight before applying strain.
- Not suitable for stiff or slippery ropes.

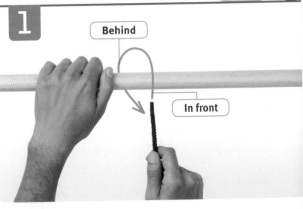

1

Behind

In front

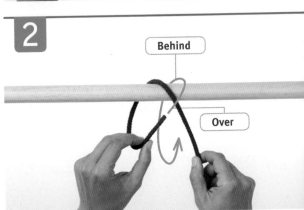

2

Behind

Over

3

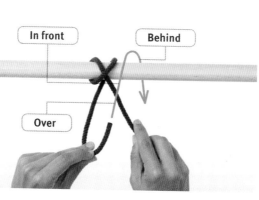

In front

Behind

Over

4

Under

5

Tighten to finish

Locked pull

Round Turn and Two Half Hitches

- Used to secure a rope to a fixed object, such as a pole or ring.
- Easy to tie.
- Ensure that you make the half hitches (*see p.23*) in the same direction.

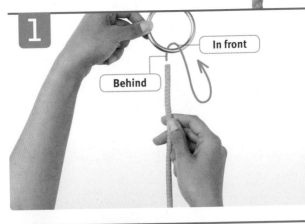

1

In front

Behind

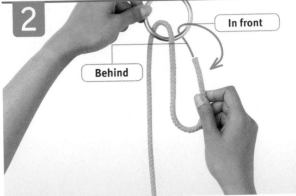

2

In front

Behind

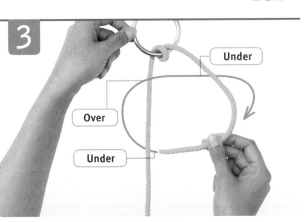

3

Under
Over
Under

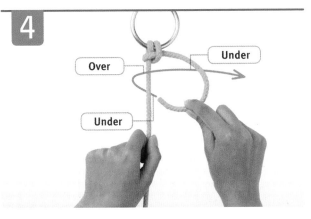

4

Over
Under
Under

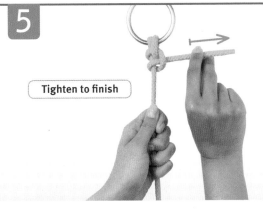

5

Tighten to finish

Buntline Hitch

- Used to attach a rope to an object such as a ring or pole.
- Will not come undone even when subjected to a lot of movement.
- Works well with hi-tech rope, such as Kevlar.

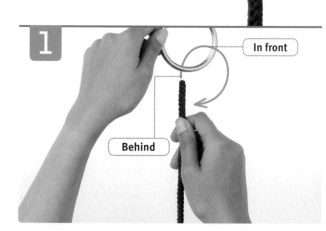

1

In front

Behind

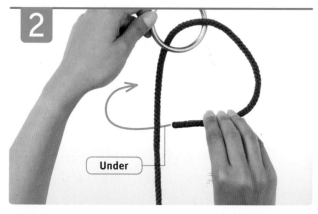

2

Under

3

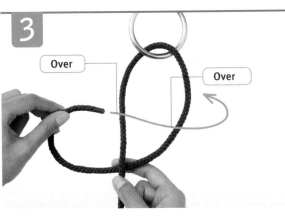

Over

Over

4

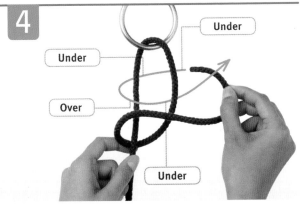

Under

Under

Over

Under

5

Tighten to finish

Fisherman's Bend

- Good for tying a rope to an anchor or a buoy.
- Easy to untie.
- Seize (*see pp.387–89*) the working end to the standing part to make more secure.
- Also known as the Anchor Bend.

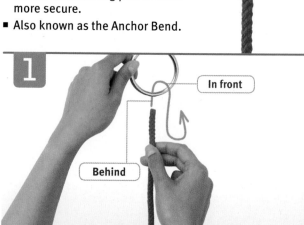

1

In front

Behind

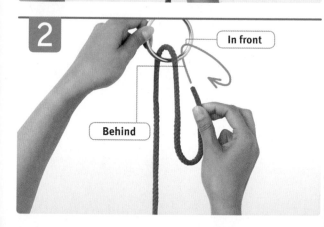

2

In front

Behind

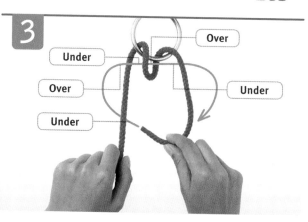

3

Over
Under
Over
Under
Under

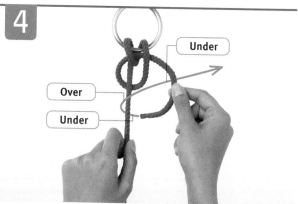

4

Under
Over
Under

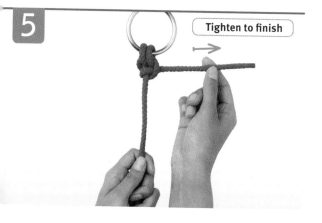

5

Tighten to finish

BEST FOR ...
Camping

A few simple knots can make camping much easier
and safer. They can be helpful in pitching a tent and
transporting equipment and, in survival situations, can
be used to make a shelter or lash a tarpaulin to trees.

Rolling Hitch » pp.176–77

☑ A hitch that can be used
to secure guy ropes to a
tent peg.

☑ Can be used to apply
tension to a line if your
guy ropes do not have an
adjuster.

☑ Strain can be applied
horizontally in one
direction, or vertically.

Similar knots:
» pp.178–79
**Mirrored
Rolling Hitch**

Sheer Lashing
» pp.222–24

☑ A lashing that is perfect
for making the frame
of a shelter.

☑ Can also be used to
attach a reinforcing piece
of wood to a broken pole.

☑ If tied loosely at the end
of two poles, it can be
opened out into an A-frame.

Similar knots:
» pp.211–14
Square Lashing

Square Lashing
>> pp.211–14

✅ A good multi-purpose, load-bearing lashing used to tie two poles together at right angles.

✅ Can be used to build rigid structures of all sizes – useful for a temporary table or stand while camping.

Similar knots:
**>> pp.215–17
Diagonal Lashing**

Round Turn and Two Half Hitches **>> pp.180–81**

✅ The perfect knot for attaching a line to a ring, pole, or post.

✅ Can support heavy loads, so is ideal for fastening a rope swing to a branch of a tree.

✅ Can also be used to secure a guy rope to a tent peg.

Similar knots:
**>> pp.184–85
Fisherman's Bend**

Bowline **>> pp.240–41**

✅ A simple knot for tying a loop around a fixed object.

✅ Good for tying tarpaulins or sheets – it won't slip or jam easily in windy conditions.

✅ Can also be used to hang a hammock, or attach a canoe to a trailer.

Similar knots:
**>> pp.245–47
Bowline with
Two Turns
>> pp.249–52
Figure-of-Eight
Loop**

Waggoner's Hitch
» pp.203–04

✓ Used for centuries to fasten loads onto wagons and trucks, it will secure a load tightly to a roof rack or trailer.

✓ Use where a rope needs to be pulled extra tight – the knot's lever-type action allows strain to be put on a rope.

Similar knots:
**» pp.211–14
Square Lashing
» pp.222–24
Sheer Lashing**

Cow Hitch

- Used to tie a rope around a ring or pole.
- Formed with two half hitches (*see p.23*) tied in opposite directions.
- The least secure of all hitches unless used with a fixed loop.
- Also known as the Lark's Head.

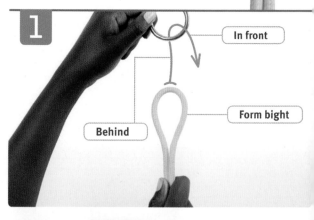

1

In front

Behind

Form bight

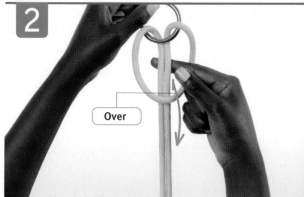

2

Over

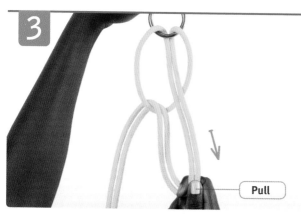

3

Pull

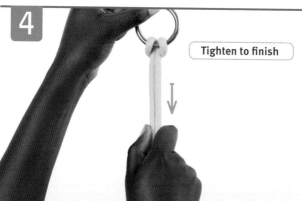

4

Tighten to finish

Pedigree Cow Hitch

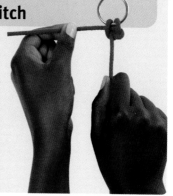

- If only one standing part of a Cow Hitch (*see pp.190–91*) is taking strain, make it more secure by tucking the other part between the bight and ring.

- Ensure the tail is long, so it does not pull out if strain is applied.

Cow Hitch with Toggle

- Variation of a Cow Hitch (*see pp.190–91*) used when there is no access to the working end of the rope.
- Remove the toggle for quick release.

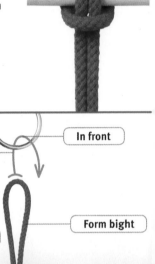

1

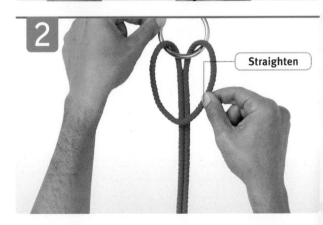

In front

Behind

Form bight

2

Straighten

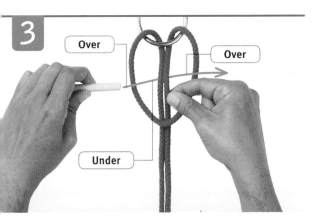

3

Over

Over

Under

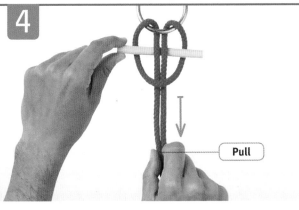

4

Pull

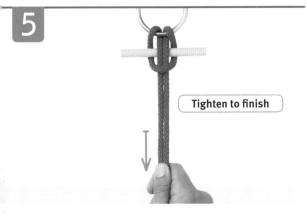

5

Tighten to finish

Sheepshank

- Used to shorten a rope without cutting it and to relieve the strain on worn-out parts of a rope.
- Ensure that the rope is taut to avoid slackening of the knot.
- Seize (*see pp.387–89*) the end loops to the standing parts of the rope for greater security.

1

Cross under twice

Cross under

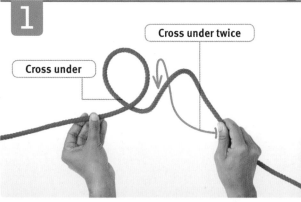

2

Reach through and grip

3

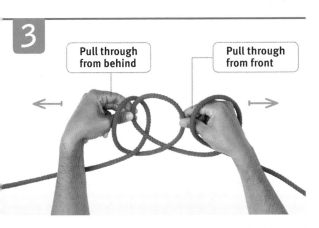

Pull through from behind

Pull through from front

4

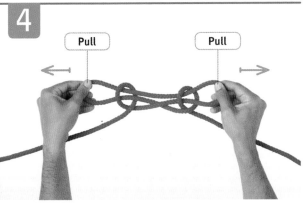

Pull

Pull

5

Tighten to finish

Sheepshank Man o' War

- Used to shorten a rope or to relieve tension on a worn-out part of rope.
- A secure version of the Sheepshank (*see pp.194–95*) that is easy to untie.
- Made with four half hitches (*see p.23*).
- Seize (*see pp.387–89*) the end loops to the standing parts for greater security.

1

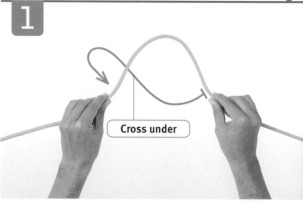

Cross under

2

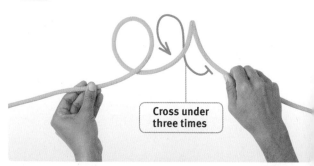

Cross under three times

3

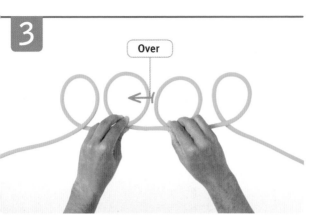

Over

4

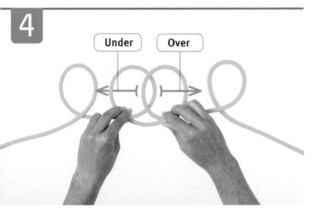

Under   Over

5

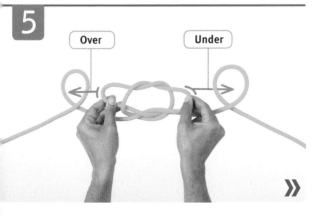

Over   Under

»

6

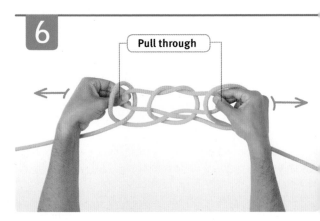

Pull through

7

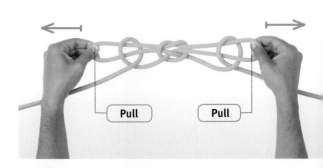

Pull   Pull

8

Tighten to finish

Marlinespike Hitch

- Useful for pulling on a thin line or rope.
- Quick and easy to tie – the knot disappears when the spike is removed.
- Can only be pulled in one direction.
- A marlinespike (*see p.19*) is not essential – will work with any type of rod or spike.

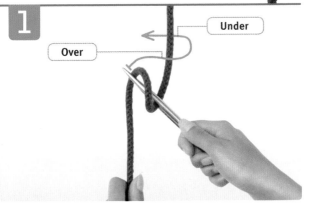

Under

Over

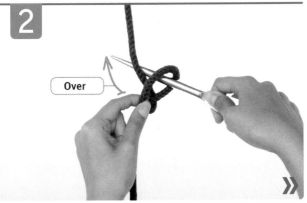

Over

»

3

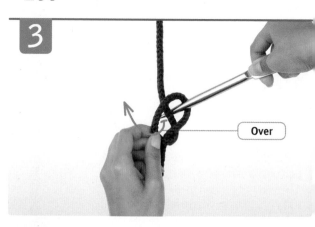

Over

4

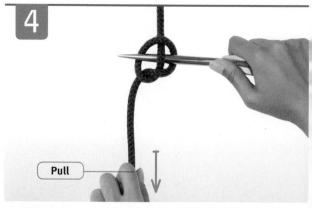

Pull

5

Tighten to finish

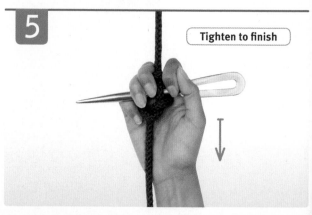

Highwayman's Hitch

- A quick-release hitch.
- Used to tether horses.
- Ensure that the strain is placed on the standing part.
- Pull the short end to release.

1

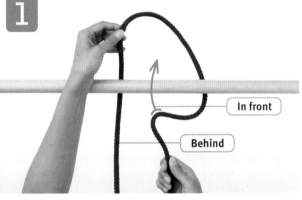

In front

Behind

2

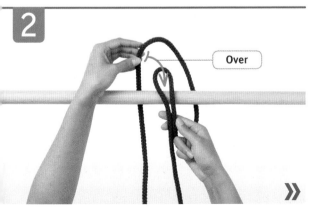

Over

»

3

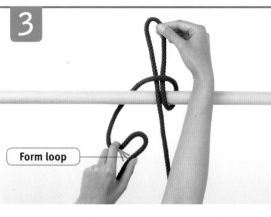

Form loop

4

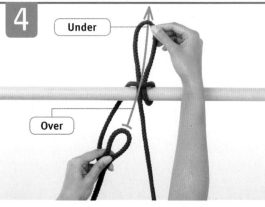

Under

Over

5

Tighten to finish

Waggoner's Hitch

- Allows strain to be put on a length of rope.
- Traditionally used to secure loads on wagons and lorries.
- Will come undone as soon as the tension is removed.
- Constant use of this hitch in the same place on the rope can lead to rapid wear.

1

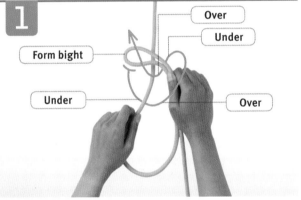

Over

Under

Form bight

Under

Over

2

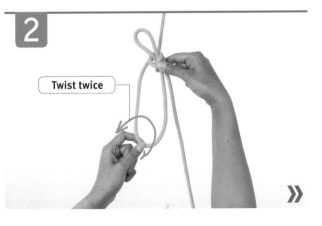

Twist twice

»

3

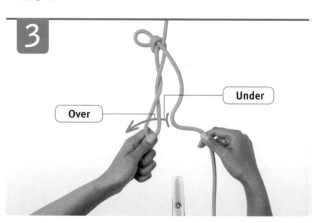

Over

Under

4

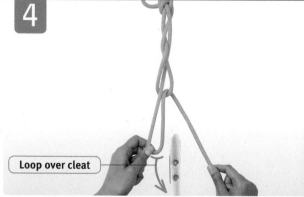

Loop over cleat

5

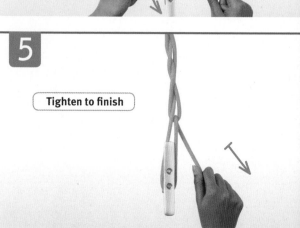

Tighten to finish

Snelling a Hook

- Used to bind a fishing line to a hook.
- Can also be used to attach a line to a hook without an eye, known as a spade-ended hook.
- Moisten the nylon line to help draw it tight.

1

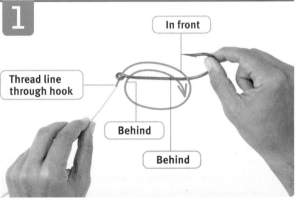

Thread line through hook

In front

Behind

Behind

2

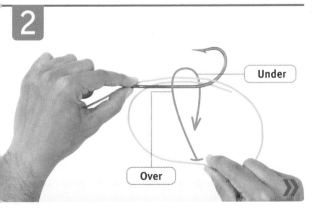

Under

Over

3

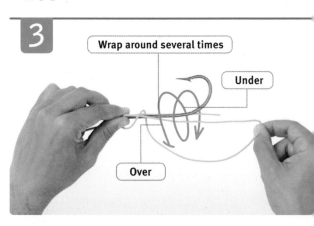

Wrap around several times

Under

Over

4

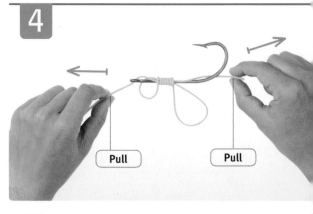

Pull

Pull

5

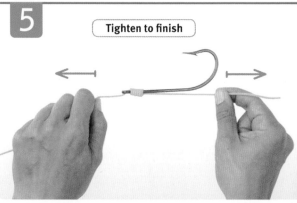

Tighten to finish

Clinch Knot

- Used to tie fishing line to the eye of a hook.
- For thicker lines, wrap around four times only.
- Moisten the line before working the knot into shape.

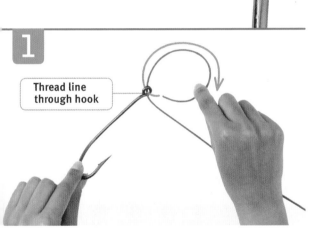

1

Thread line through hook

2

Wrap around at least six times

Over

Under

»

3

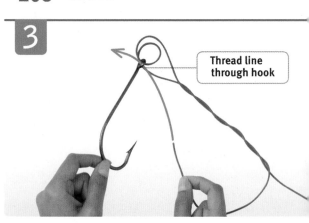

Thread line through hook

4

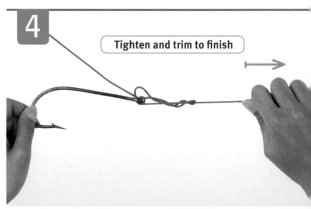

Tighten and trim to finish

Improved Clinch Knot

- Used for particularly thin and slippery fishing line.
- The extra tuck gives additional security and prevents the knot from coming undone.

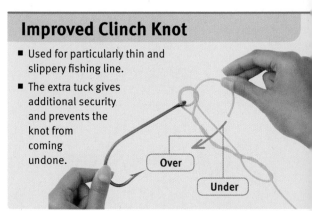

Over

Under

Palomar Knot

- Used to secure a fishing line to a hook or lure.
- A strong knot that works with slippery nylon line.
- Difficult to untie.
- Moisten the line to help draw it tight.

1

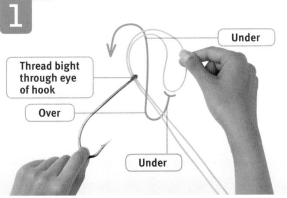

Under

Thread bight through eye of hook

Over

Under

2

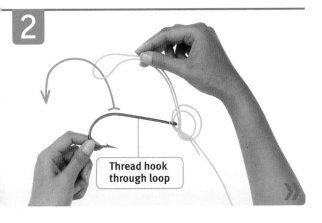

Thread hook through loop

3

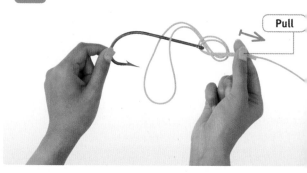

Pull

4

Pull

5

Tighten to finish

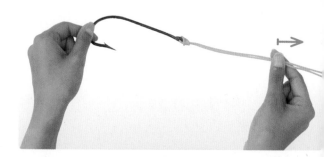

Square Lashing

- Used to lash together two poles crossing at right angles.
- Pull tight each turn before proceeding to the next one.
- Start and finish with a Clove Hitch (*see pp.105–06*).
- Ensure that the first Clove Hitch is tied below the horizontal pole.
- Tighten by making two turns across the lashing (frapping turns).

1 TIE A CLOVE HITCH (»pp.105–06)

Behind

2

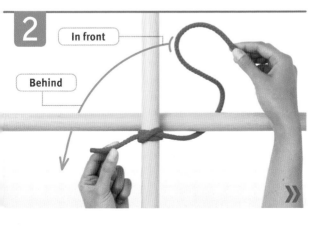

In front

Behind

»

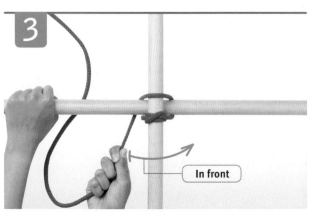

3

In front

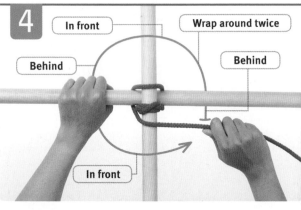

4

In front

Wrap around twice

Behind

Behind

In front

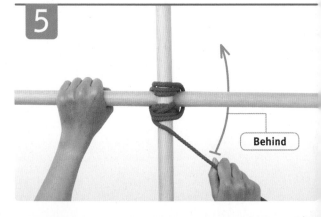

5

Behind

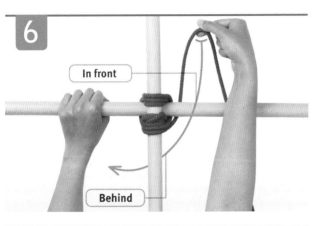

6

In front

Behind

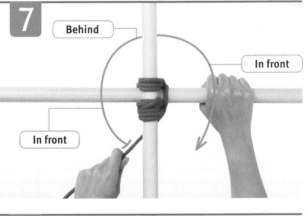

7

Behind

In front

In front

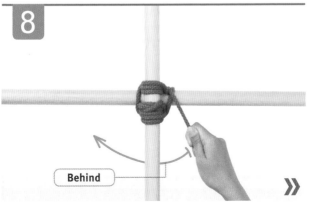

8

Behind

»

9

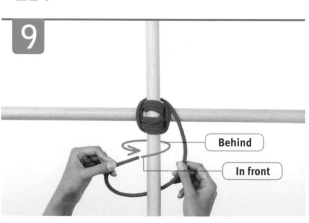

Behind

In front

10

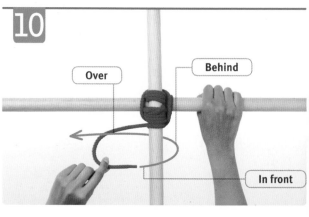

Over

Behind

In front

11

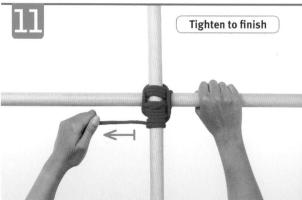

Tighten to finish

Diagonal Lashing

- Used to lash together two diagonal poles.
- Before you start, ensure there is enough rope to complete the lashing.
- Tighten with two turns across the lashing (frapping turns).
- Finish with a Clove Hitch (*see pp.105–06*).

1   TIE A TIMBER HITCH (»pp.111–13)

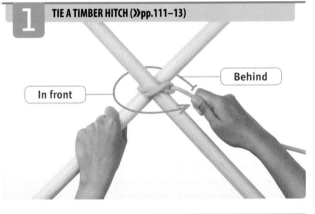

In front

Behind

2

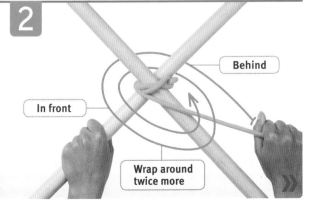

Behind

In front

Wrap around twice more

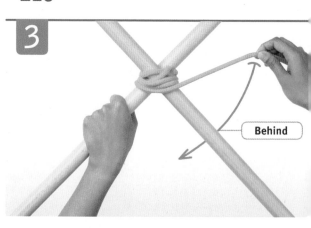

3

Behind

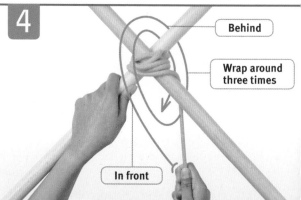

4

Behind

Wrap around three times

In front

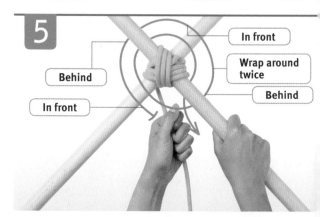

5

In front

Wrap around twice

Behind

Behind

In front

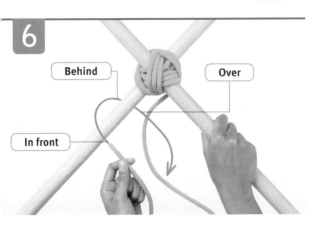

6

Behind

Over

In front

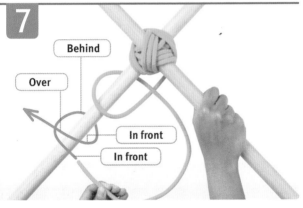

7

Behind

Over

In front

In front

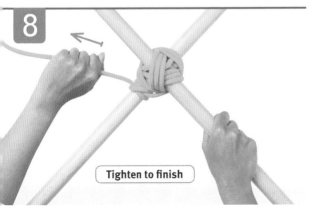

8

Tighten to finish

BEST FOR ...
Gardening

There are several uses for knots around the garden, from simple jobs like tying a plant to a support, to bigger tasks such as lashing canes together to make a trellis or fixing a swing to a tree.

Constrictor Knot
>> pp.109–10

✓ Good for fixing a hose in position if you do not have a hose clip.

✓ Can also be used to draw together a bundle of objects such as logs.

✗ Difficult to untie once it has been put under strain – it may need to be cut.

Similar knots:
>> pp.105–06
Clove Hitch
>> pp.114–16
Boa Knot

Sheer Lashing
>> pp.222–23

✓ The perfect knot for tying two canes together to make a support for a plant.

✓ Can also be used with thinner line to tie a sapling to a support post.

Similar knots:
>> pp.211–14
Square Lashing
>> pp.215–17
Diagonal Lashing

Round Turn and Two Half Hitches »pp.180–81

✓ Useful for tying a line to a ring or post.

✓ Can also be used to tie a swing to a tree branch.

✗ If used for a swing, padding may need to be placed under the rope to protect the tree.

Similar knots:
» pp.182–83
Buntline Hitch
» pp.184–85
Fisherman's Bend

Square Lashing
»pp.211–14

✓ Good for making support frames for vegetables such as beans or tomatoes.

✓ Can also be used to make a trellis.

✓ Add frapping turns to make the knot more secure.

Similar knots:
» pp.215–17
Diagonal Lashing
» pp.222–23
Sheer Lashing

Timber Hitch
》 p.111–13

✅ A good hitch for tying up bundles of branches, as its tightening action increases with strain.

✅ Can be finished with a half hitch for extra security when dragging larger loads, or transporting a bundle over a long distance.

Similar knots:
**》 pp.109–10
Constrictor
Knot**

Sheet Bend
》 pp.140–41

✅ Best used for joining ropes together because it is quick and easy to tie, and unlikely to untie accidentally.

❌ A Double Sheet Bend is required when joining ropes of different diameters.

Similar knots:
**》 pp.105–06
Clove Hitch
》 pp.144–45
Double Sheet Bend
》 pp.157–59
Fisherman's Knot**

Sheer Lashing

- Used for lashing together adjacent poles.
- Also used to reinforce a weak pole.
- Tighten by making two turns across the lashing (frapping turns).
- Start and finish with a Clove Hitch (*see pp.105–06*).
- Ensure the first Clove Hitch is tied around both poles.

1 TIE A CLOVE HITCH (»pp.105–06)

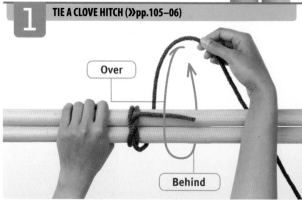

Over

Behind

2

Wrap around several times

Over

Behind

3

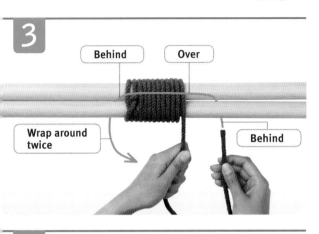

Behind | Over

Wrap around twice

Behind

4

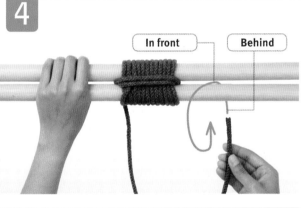

In front | Behind

5

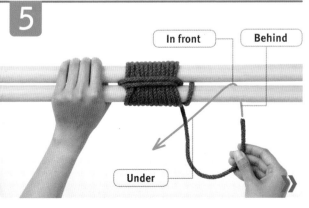

In front | Behind

Under

6

Behind

7

Tighten to finish

A-Frame Lashing

- Follows the same process as a Sheer Lashing (*see pp.222–24*).
- Can be used to form the legs of a rope bridge.
- Make the turns looser, so the poles can be pulled into an "A" shape.

Icicle Hitch

- More grip than the Rolling Hitch (*see pp.176–77*).
- Good for use on slippery surfaces.
- For additional grip, add extra turns at the start of the knot.
- Ensure that the first series of turns are locked under the diagonal turn.
- For increased security, hold the line with your hand as strain is applied.

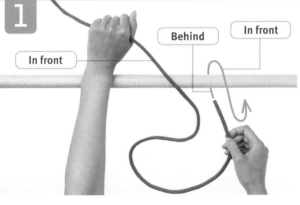

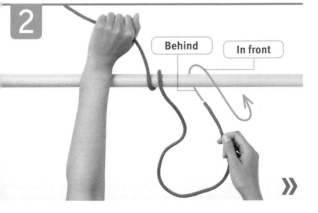

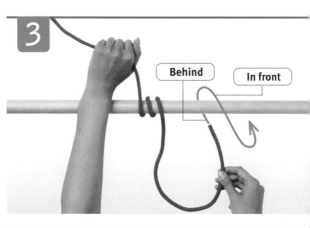

3

Behind | In front

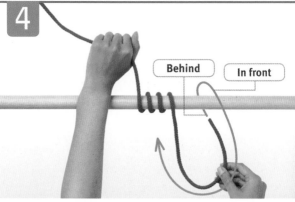

4

Behind | In front

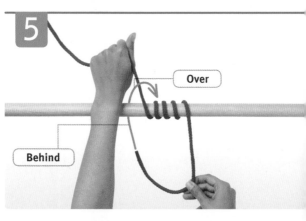

5

Over

Behind

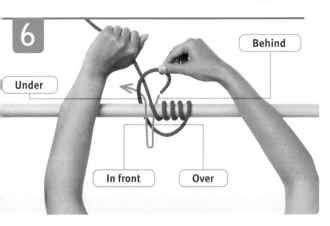

6

Behind

Under

In front   Over

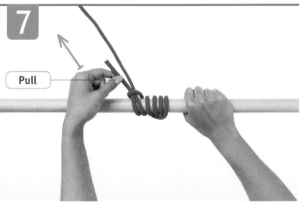

7

Pull

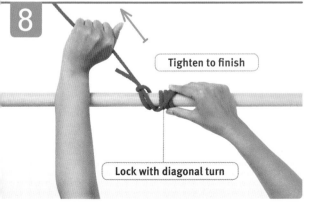

8

Tighten to finish

Lock with diagonal turn

Prusik Knot

- Used to attach a climbing sling to a main rope.
- Will slide up and down the main rope when strain is removed.
- Sling should be half the diameter of the main rope at most.
- Created in 1931 by Dr Carl Prusik, an Austrian mountaineer.

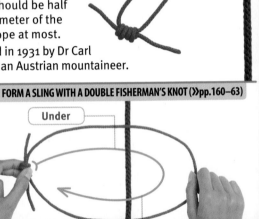

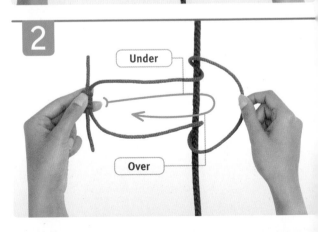

1 — FORM A SLING WITH A DOUBLE FISHERMAN'S KNOT (≫pp.160–63)

Under

Over

2

Under

Over

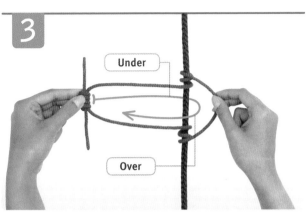

3

Under

Over

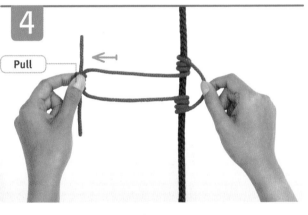

4

Pull

5

Tighten to finish

Bachmann Knot

- Used by climbers to ascend a fixed rope.
- Grips the rope tightly when loaded.
- Strain should only be applied to the sling, not the karabiner.
- Use the karabiner to move up and down the rope when there is no strain on the sling.

1 FORM A SLING WITH A DOUBLE FISHERMAN'S KNOT (»pp.160–63)

Place in karabiner

2

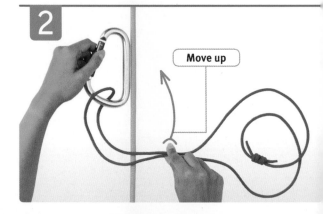

Move up

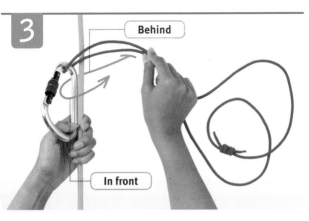

3

Behind

In front

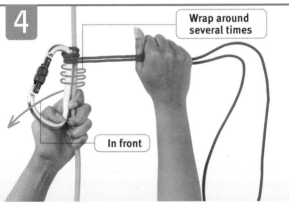

4

Wrap around several times

In front

5

Tighten to finish

Klemheist Knot

- A variation of the Prusik Knot (*see pp.228–29*) that can be used for moving up or down a climbing rope.
- Soft tubular climbing tape can be used to form the sling.
- The rope used to form the sling should be at least half the diameter of the main rope.

1 FORM A SLING WITH A DOUBLE FISHERMAN'S KNOT (≫pp.160–63)

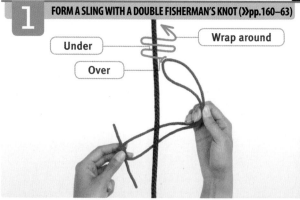

Under

Wrap around

Over

2

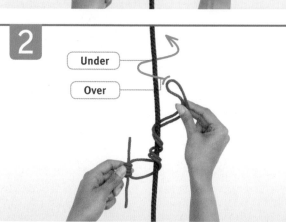

Under

Over

3

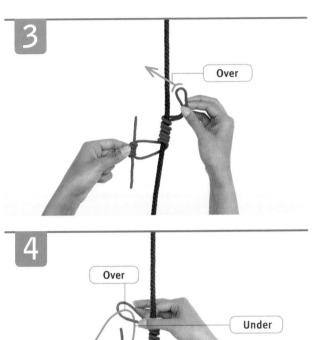

Over

4

Over

Under

5

Tighten to finish

Italian Hitch

- A sliding hitch used in climbing and abseiling to control a descent.
- Pull on the loaded rope (rope that takes the strain) to cause the knot to slip.
- Pull on the braking rope to control the speed of the slip.
- The braking rope should not be confused with the loaded rope.

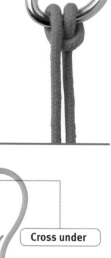

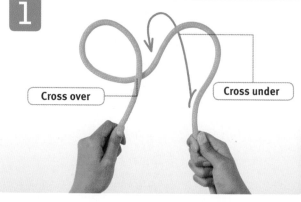

1

Cross over · Cross under

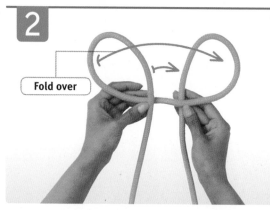

2

Fold over

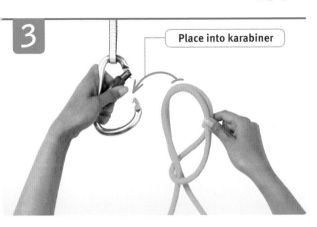

3 Place into karabiner

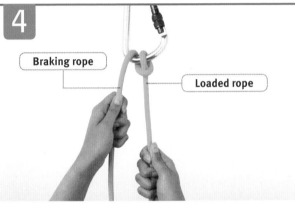

4 Braking rope | Loaded rope

Reversed Italian Hitch

- In the Reversed Italian Hitch, the loaded rope and the braking rope are reversed.
- The braking rope becomes the loaded rope, and vice versa.

Braking rope

Loaded rope

Loops

A loop knot can be used to secure a rope to an object, such as a hook or a ring, or may even be tied around a person's wrist or waist. Loop knots can also be used to join two separate ropes of different thicknesses.

Alpine Butterfly

- Used by climbers to secure themselves to the middle of a rope.
- Will take strain in either direction.
- Can be tied quickly.

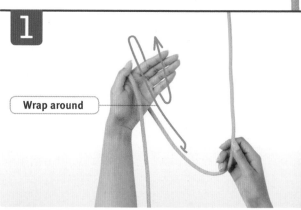

1

Wrap around

2

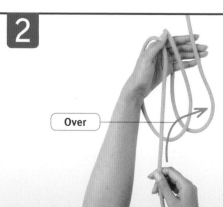

Over

3

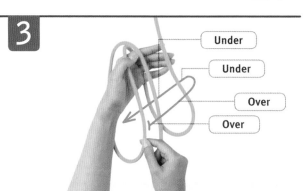

- Under
- Under
- Over
- Over

4

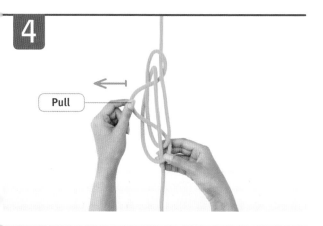

Pull

5

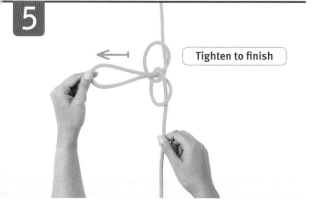

Tighten to finish

Bowline

- A widely used, general-purpose loop knot.
- Easy to tie and untie.
- Ensure that the finished knot has a good tail.
- Can be tied in two ways (*see pp.242–44*) – use this method when the standing part is free.

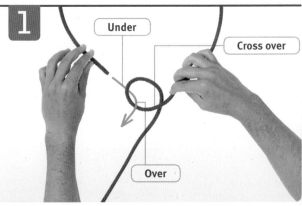

1

Under

Cross over

Over

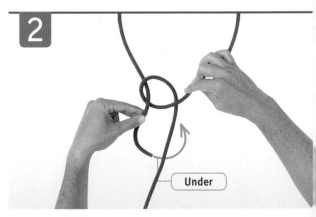

2

Under

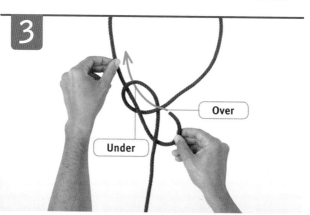

3

Under
Over

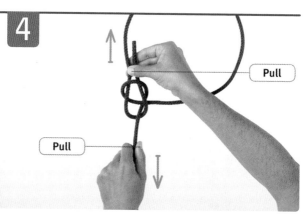

4

Pull
Pull

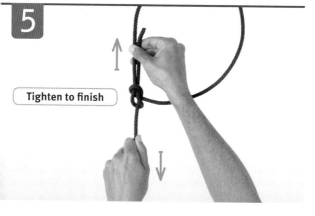

5

Tighten to finish

Bowline – Second Method

- Used to tie a loop around the waist for activities such as sailing and climbing.
- Ensure that the loop has a good tail (short end).
- Best method for tying a Bowline (*see pp.240–41*) if the standing end of the rope is fixed.

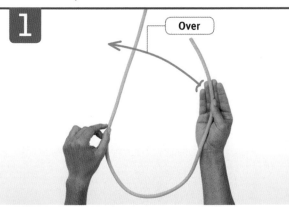

1 Over

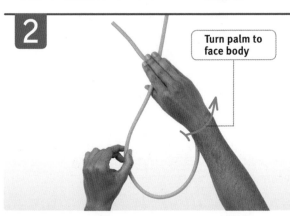

2 Turn palm to face body

3

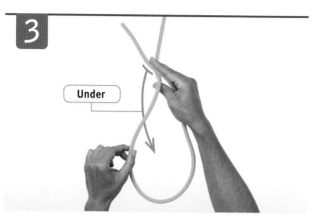

Under

4

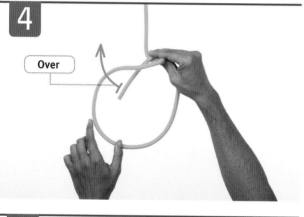

Over

5

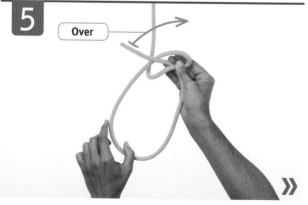

Over

»

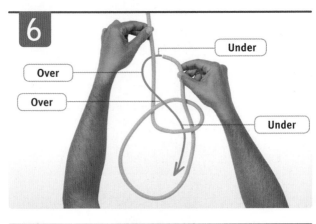

6

Under
Over
Over
Under

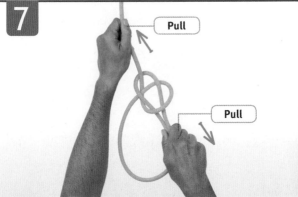

7

Pull
Pull

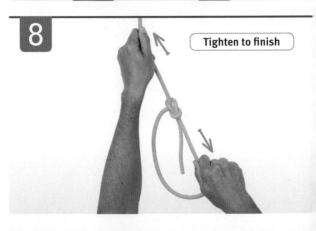

8

Tighten to finish

Bowline with Two Turns

- A more secure version of a Bowline (*see pp.240–43*) tied with an extra turn.
- Ensure the finished knot has a good tail (working end).

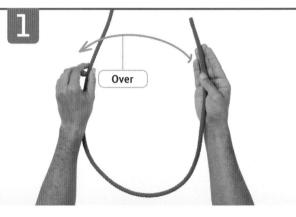

1

Over

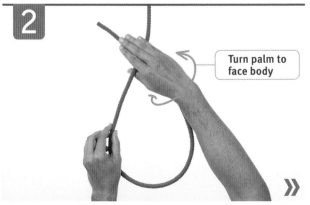

2

Turn palm to face body

》

3

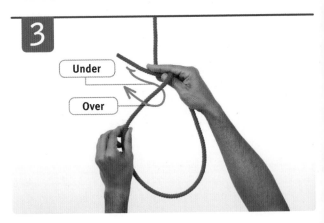

Under

Over

4

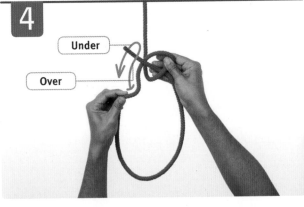

Under

Over

5

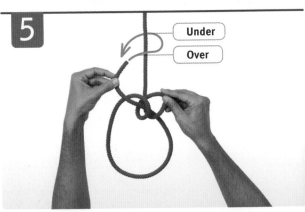

Under

Over

6

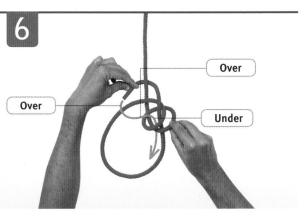

Over

Over

Under

7

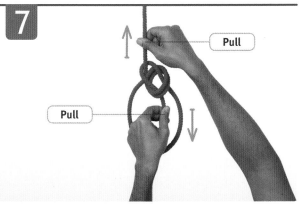

Pull

Pull

8

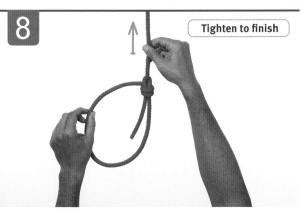

Tighten to finish

Bowline with Stopper

- A secure version of the Bowline (*see pp.240–43*) that is popular with climbers.
- Working end is tied around the loop using the Overhand Knot (*see pp.28–29*).

1 TIE A BOWLINE (»pp.240–43)

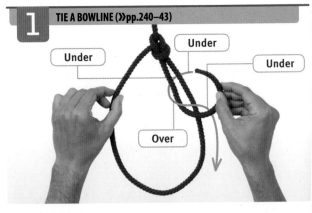

Under

Under

Under

Over

2

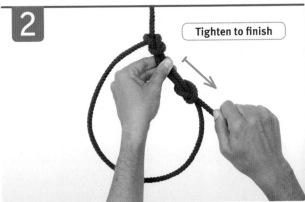

Tighten to finish

Figure-of-Eight Loop

- A popular climber's loop that can take a moderate amount of strain.
- Distinctive shape makes it easy to check if the knot is secure.
- Can be tied in fine nylon.
- Also known as the Double Figure-of-Eight Knot.

1

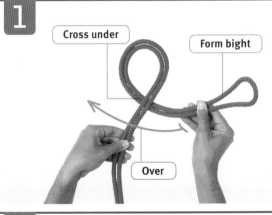

Cross under

Form bight

Over

2

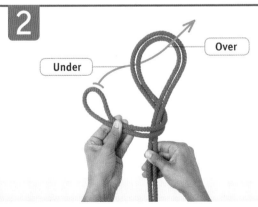

Under

Over

»

3

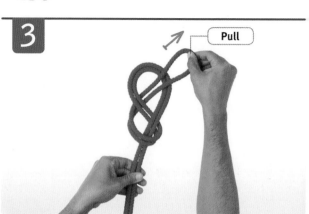

Pull

4

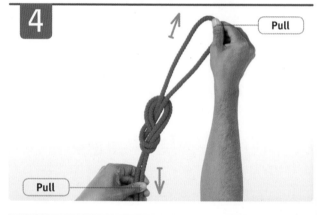

Pull

Pull

5

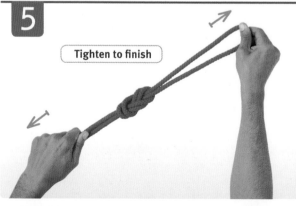

Tighten to finish

Threaded Figure-of-Eight Loop

- A Figure-of-Eight Loop (*see pp.249–50*) that can be threaded through a ring.
- Used for attaching climbing rope to a harness.
- The finished knot should be neat and snug.
- Not as easy to untie as the Bowline (*see pp.240–41*).

1 TIE A FIGURE OF EIGHT (》pp.38–39)

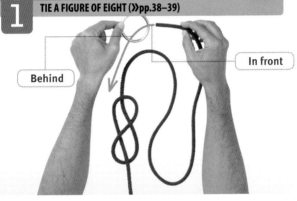

Behind

In front

2

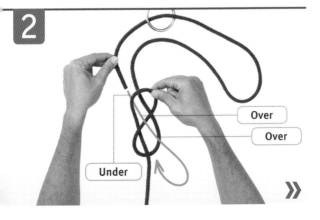

Over

Over

Under

》

3

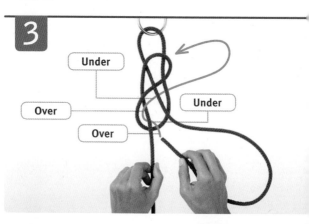

Under

Over

Under

Over

4

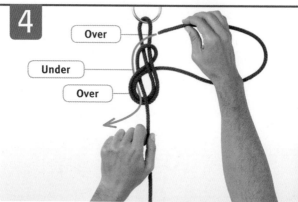

Over

Under

Over

5

Tighten to finish

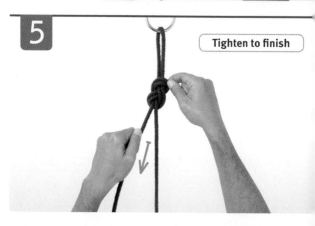

Overhand Loop

- A simple method for creating a fixed loop.
- Made from an Overhand Knot (*see pp.28–29*) tied in the bight.
- Difficult to untie.

1

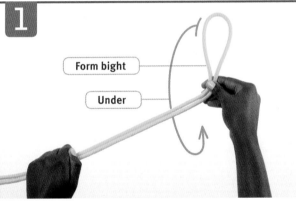

Form bight

Under

2

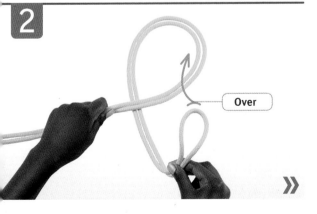

Over

»

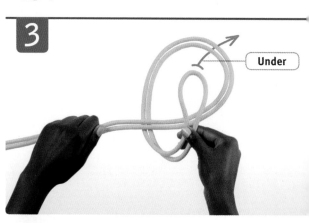

3

Under

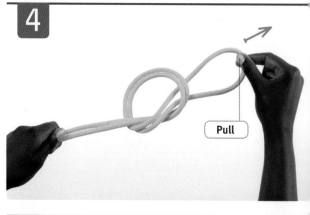

4

Pull

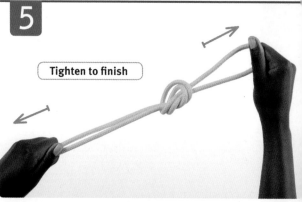

5

Tighten to finish

Double Overhand Loop

- A loop knot suitable for all types of thin ropes and cords, such as fishing line.
- Tied using the same method as the Double Overhand Knot (*see pp.32–33*), but with a doubled length of rope.
- Can be difficult to untie.

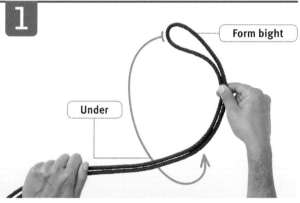

1

Form bight

Under

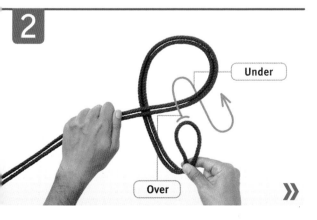

2

Under

Over

»

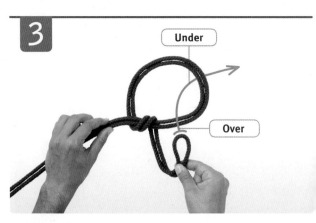

3

Under

Over

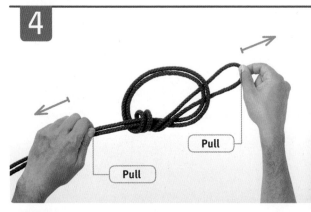

4

Pull

Pull

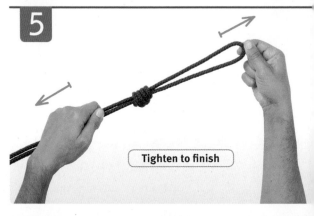

5

Tighten to finish

Double Overhand Sliding Loop

- Good for attaching a fishing line to a hook or a cord to a pair of spectacles.
- Work the knot into a neat shape to ensure it slides easily.

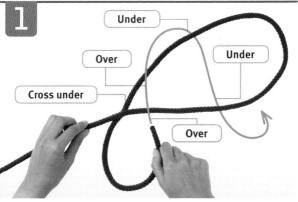

1

Under

Under

Over

Under

Cross under

Over

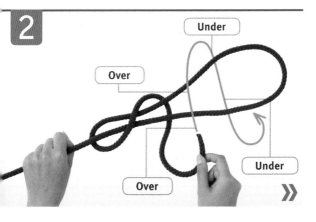

2

Under

Over

Over

Under

»

3

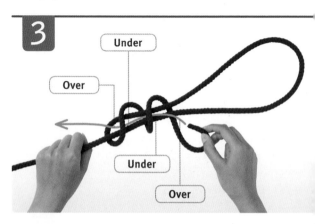

Under

Over

Under

Over

4

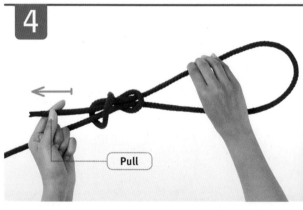

Pull

5

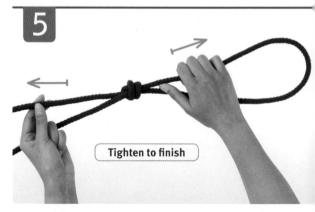

Tighten to finish

Bowline on the Bight

- A secure, double loop knot that can take strain.
- Each of the two fixed loops can be used for separate functions.
- Quick to tie and easy to untie.
- Can be tied in the middle of the rope.

1

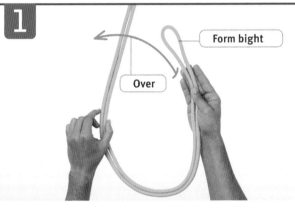

Form bight

Over

2

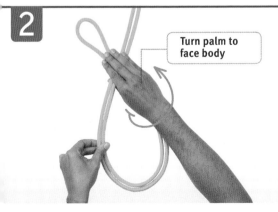

Turn palm to face body

»

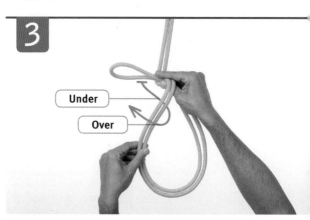

Under

Over

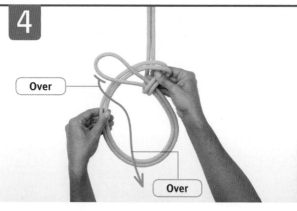

Over

Over

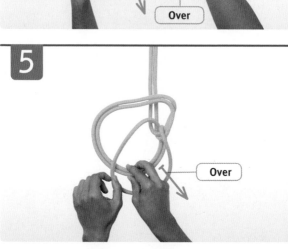

Over

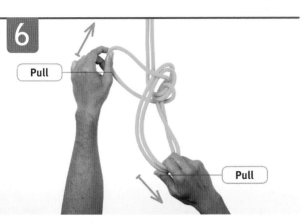

6

Pull

Pull

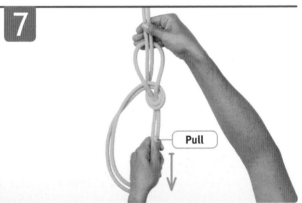

7

Pull

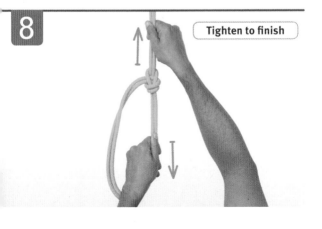

8

Tighten to finish

Portuguese Bowline

- Used to tie two adjustable loops quickly.
- Equal strain must be placed on both loops to prevent them from changing size while in use.

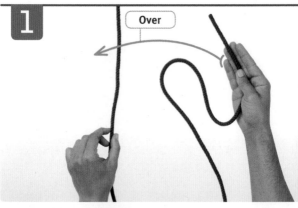

1 Over

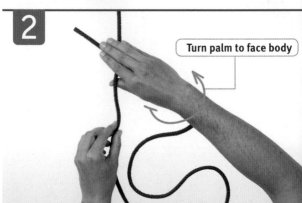

2 Turn palm to face body

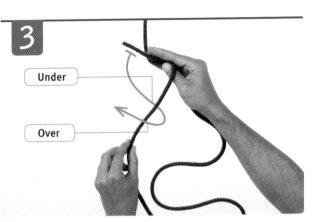

3

Under

Over

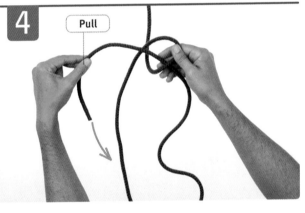

4

Pull

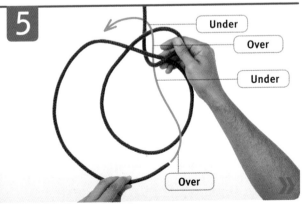

5

Under

Over

Under

Over

6

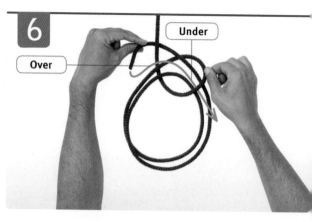

Over

Under

7

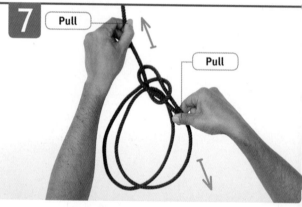

Pull

Pull

8

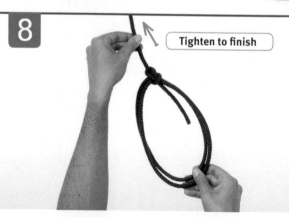

Tighten to finish

Spanish Bowline

- A variation of the Bowline (*see pp.240–43*), this knot forms two adjustable loops that lock into position.
- Can be tied in the middle of the rope.
- Place equal strain on both loops.

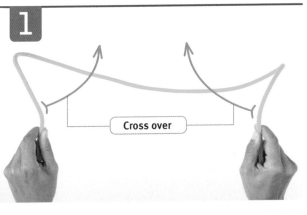

1

Cross over

2

Twist over   Twist over

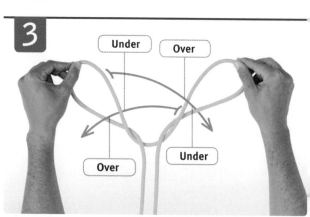

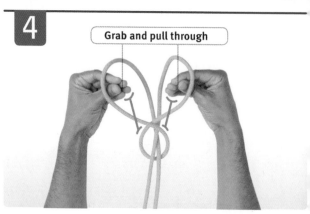

Grab and pull through

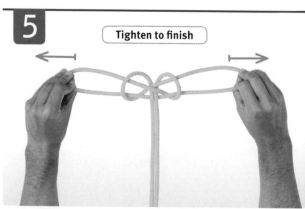

Tighten to finish

Angler's Loop

- Ideal for making a fixed loop in thin lines and ropes.
- Also works well with elasticated cord (shock cord).
- Quick to tie.
- Not suitable for thick ropes as it can be difficult to untie.

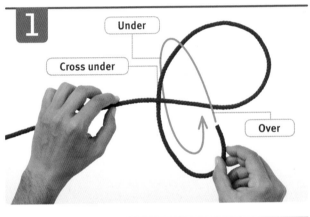

1

Under

Cross under

Over

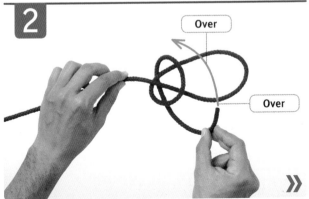

2

Over

Over

»

3

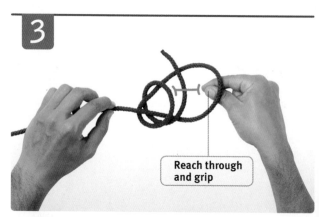

Reach through and grip

4

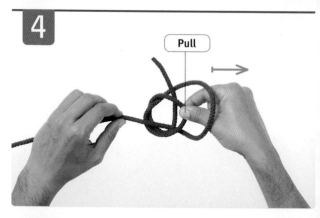

Pull

5

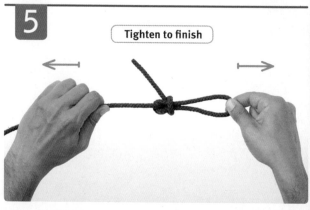

Tighten to finish

Single Figure-of-Eight Loop on the Bight

- Can be tied in the middle of the rope.
- Quick to tie and reasonably easy to untie.
- Creates a loop that can only be pulled in one direction.

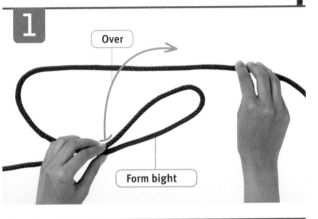

1

Over

Form bight

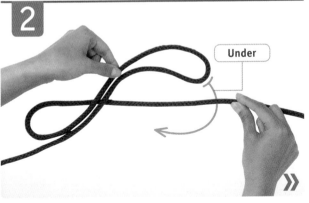

2

Under

»

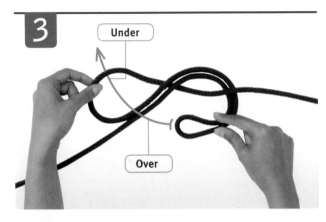

3

Under

Over

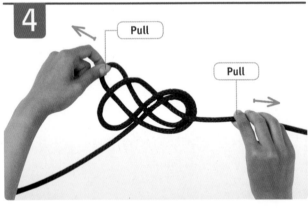

4

Pull

Pull

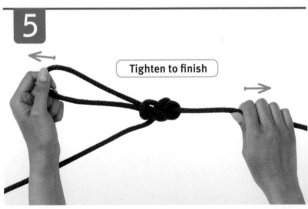

5

Tighten to finish

Englishman's Loop

- Used to form a fixed loop.
- Based on two Overhand Knots (*see pp.28–29*).
- Similar to the Fisherman's Knot (*see pp.157–59*).

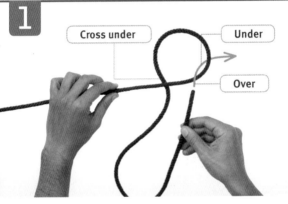

1

Cross under | Under

Over

2

Under

Over

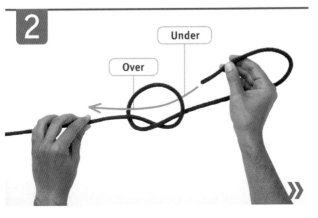

3

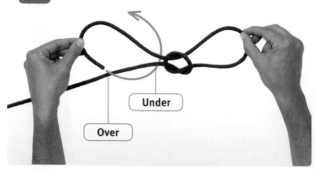

Under

Over

4

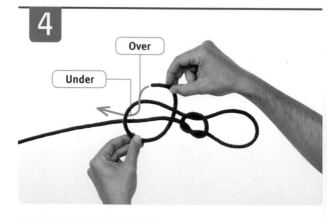

Over

Under

5

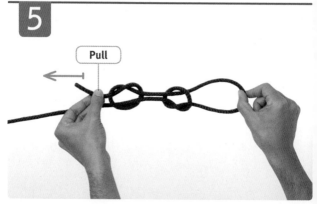

Pull

6

Bring knots together

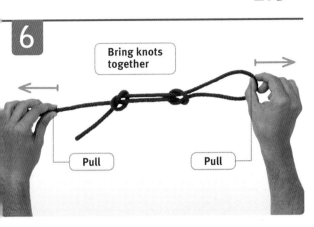

Pull | Pull

7

Tighten to finish

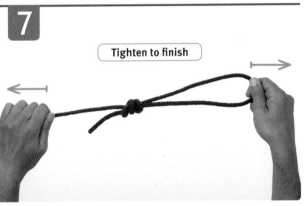

Double Englishman's Loop

- Provides extra security when used with a very slippery line.
- Simply double each Overhand Knot (see pp.28–29) tied in the Englishman's Loop (see pp.271–73).
- Use only in thin line and cords.

BEST FOR ...
Fishing

Being able to secure a line to a hook is a fundamental angling skill. It is important to remember that some fishing knots can only be used with lines of a certain thickness and material.

Palomar Knot
» pp.209–10

✓ The strongest knot for tying a fishing line to a hook –can take a great deal of strain.

✓ Will work with even the most slippery nylon line.

✓ Moistening the line will give a neater finish to the knot.

Similar knots:
» pp.205–06
Snelling a Hook
» pp.207–08
Clinch Knot

Blood Knot
» p.168–71

✓ Commonly used by anglers to join together two thin pieces of nylon line.

✓ Can take a great deal of strain.

✓ Moistening the line will help to draw the knot tight.

Similar knots:
» pp.157–59
Fisherman's Knot
» pp.160–63 Double
Fisherman's Knot

Figure-of-Eight Loop » pp.249–50

✓ A knot that is quick to tie – even with the finest fishing line.

✓ Favoured by anglers because it is easy to tie and extremely strong.

✗ Difficult to untie, especially when wet.

Similar knots:
» pp.253–54
Overhand Loop
» pp.255–58
Double Overhand Loop

Snelling a Hook
» pp.205–06

✓ A strong, neat method for tying line to a hook.

✓ Works on spade-ended hooks (hooks without an eye) as well as eyed hooks.

✓ Moistening the line will help to draw the knot tight.

Similar knots:
» p.207–08
Clinch Knot
» p.208
Improved Clinch Knot

Blood Dropper Knot
》pp.278–79

✓ A loop that allows another lure or bait to be added with a short length of line.

✓ The loop is angled away from the line, helping to prevent tangles.

Similar knots:
》pp.160–63 Double Fisherman's Knot
》p.168–71 Blood Knot

Bimini Twist 》pp.280–82

✓ A knot that makes a long strong loop in all types of fishing line.

✓ Will not slip if it has been tied correctly.

✗ Needs two people and a good deal of practice to make successfully.

Similar knots:
》pp.255–58 Double Overhand Loop
》pp.269–70 Single Figure-of-Eight Loop on the Bight

Blood Dropper Knot

- Makes a loop at the side of a line for attaching a fishing fly or lure.
- Tied at the end of the line.
- Moisten line to help draw the knot tight.

1

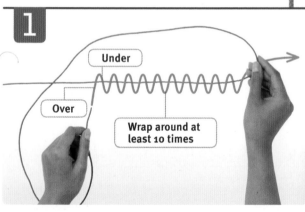

Under

Over

Wrap around at least 10 times

2

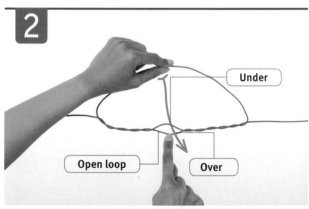

Under

Open loop

Over

3

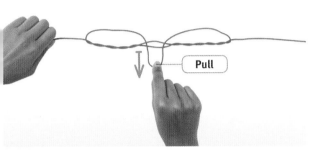

Pull

4

Pull   Pull

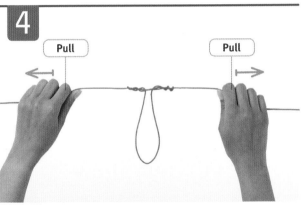

5

Tighten to finish

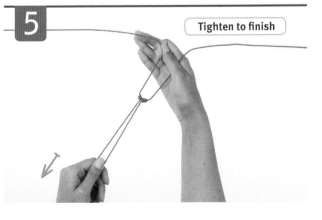

Bimini Twist

- Originally developed for use in big-game fishing.
- Suitable for both braided and monofilament fishing line.
- Forms a long, strong loop at the end of a fishing line.
- Needs practice and more than one person to tie.

1

Double the line

Twist hand clockwise

2

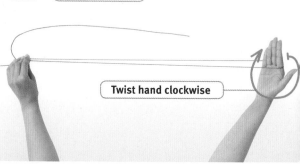

Open loop

3

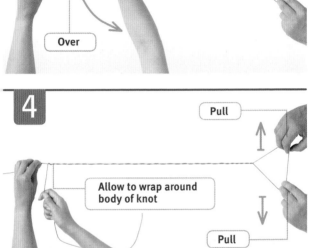

Over

4

Pull

Allow to wrap around
body of knot

Pull

5

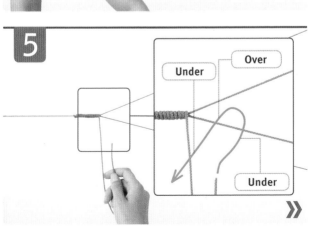

Over

Under

Under

»

6

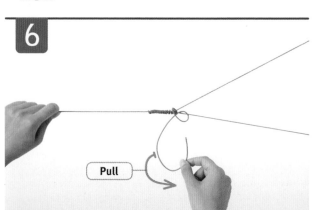

Pull

7

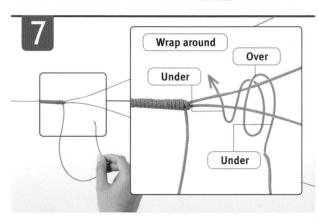

Wrap around

Over

Under

Under

8

Tighten and trim to finish

Basic Net

- A widely used technique for making and mending nets.
- Use a netting needle (see p.19, p.284) to hold the line while you work.
- Use a gauge – a piece of wood roughly half the diameter of the mesh – to ensure even spacing.

1 TIE CLOVE HITCHES (»pp.140–41) AROUND A POLE

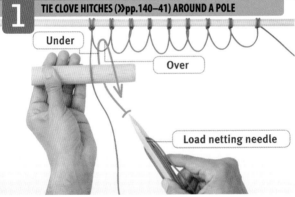

Under

Over

Load netting needle

2

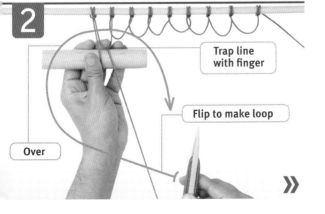

Trap line with finger

Flip to make loop

Over

»

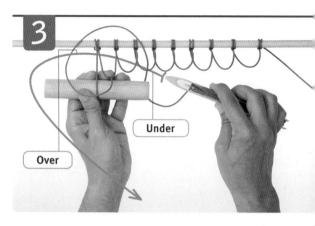

3

Over

Under

4

Repeat sequence
as required

Pull

Loading a needle

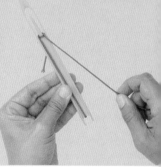

- Tie a half hitch with the
  line around the spike in
  the middle of the needle.

- Pass the long end of the
  line under the needle and
  back up the other side.

- Loop the line around
  the spike and back
  under the needle;
  repeat until finished.

Cargo Net Knot

Used to make a square net from heavy rope.

Tied with one long rope and one shorter rope.

Lay the long rope vertically and the short rope horizontally.

1

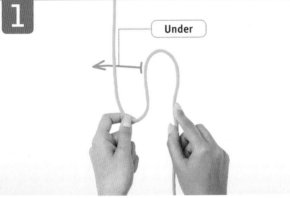

Under

2

Under

Under

Under

Over

»

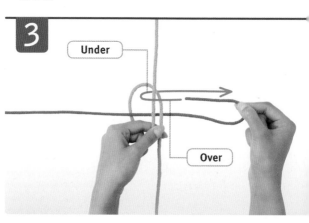

3

Under

Over

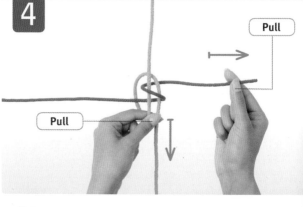

4

Pull

Pull

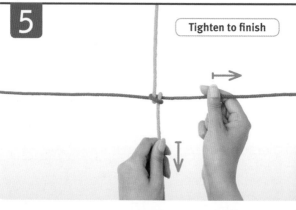

5

Tighten to finish

Jury Mast Knot

- A simple technique for tying a multiple loop knot.
- Not suitable for use in thick rope.
- Can be difficult to untie.

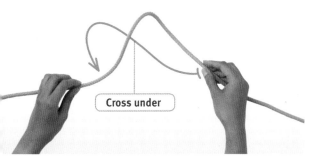

1

Cross under

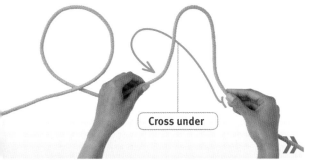

2

Cross under

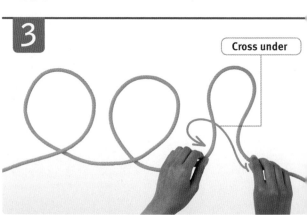

3

Cross under

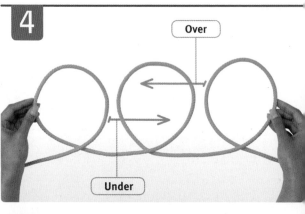

4

Over

Under

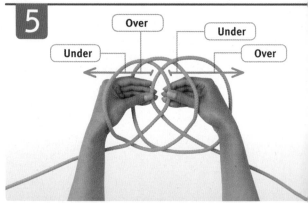

5

Over

Under

Under

Over

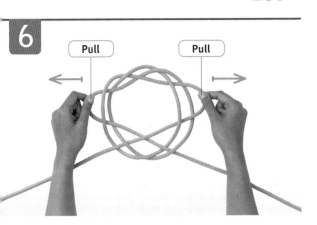

6

Pull Pull

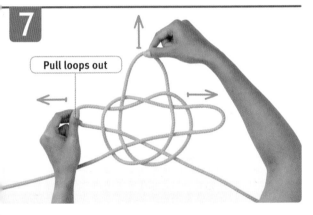

7

Pull loops out

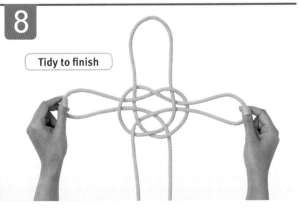

8

Tidy to finish

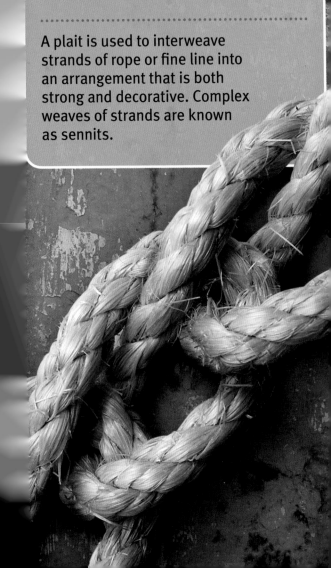

Plaits and Sennits

A plait is used to interweave strands of rope or fine line into an arrangement that is both strong and decorative. Complex weaves of strands are known as sennits.

Three-Strand Flat Plait

- The simplest of plaits.
- Bind one end of the strands together (*see pp.374–75*) before starting.
- Move alternate outer strands to the middle of the plait.
- Keep all the strands flat and tight as you plait.

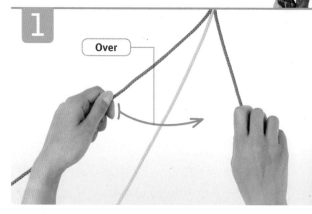

1

Over

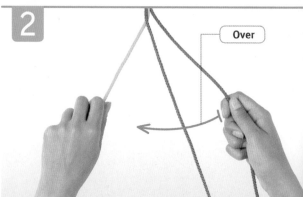

2

Over

3

Over

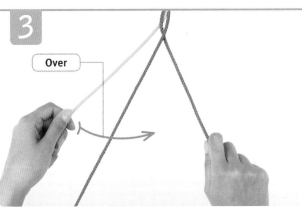

4

Repeat sequence
as required

Over

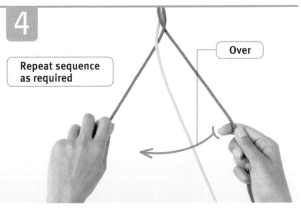

5 **WHIP (»pp.374–75) STRANDS TOGETHER TO FINISH**

Four-Strand Flat Plait

- Forms an asymmetric flat plait.
- More decorative than the Three-Strand Flat Plait (*see pp.292–93*).
- Bind one end of the strands together (*see pp.374–75*) before starting.
- Keep all the strands flat and tight as you plait.

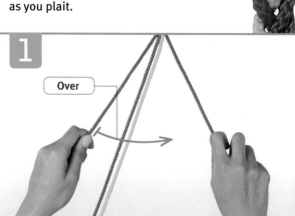

Over

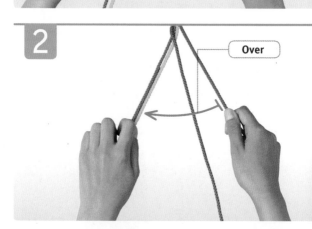

Over

3

Over

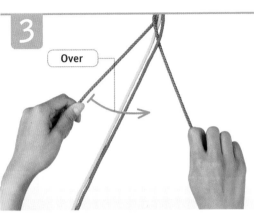

4

Repeat sequence as required

Over

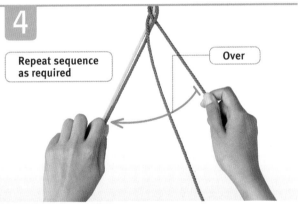

5 WHIP (»pp.374–75) STRANDS TOGETHER TO FINISH

Five-Strand Flat Plait

- Move alternate outer strands to the middle of the plait.
- Bind one end of the strands together (*see pp.374–75*) before starting.
- Keep all the strands flat and tight as you plait.

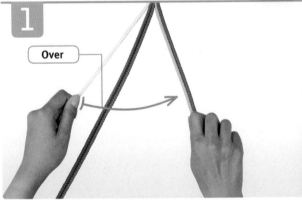

Over

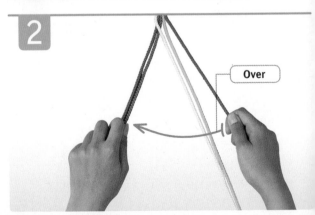

Over

3

Over

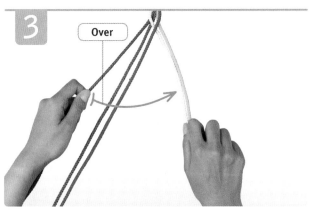

4

Repeat sequence as required

Over

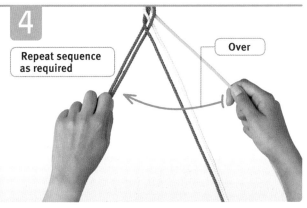

5 WHIP (»pp.374–75) STRANDS TOGETHER TO FINISH

Six-Strand Flat Plait

- Forms a large, asymmetrical decorative plait.
- Bind one end of the strands together (*see pp.374–75*) before starting.
- Keep all the strands flat and tight as you plait.

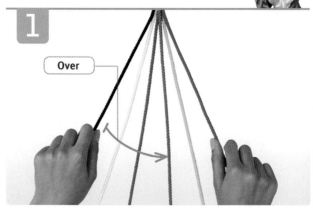

Over

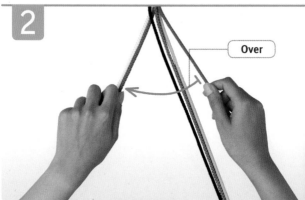

Over

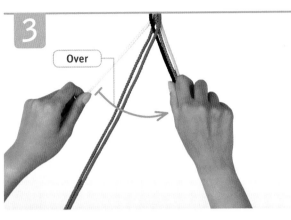

3

Over

4

Repeat sequence as required

Over

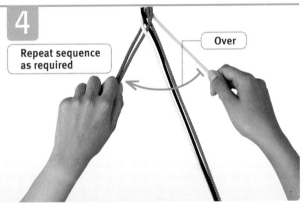

5 WHIP (»pp.374–75) STRANDS TOGETHER TO FINISH

Seven-Strand Flat Plait

- Used to form a large decorative plait.
- The largest number of strands with which it is practical to make a plait.
- Bind one end of the strands together (*see pp.374–75*) before starting.
- Keep all the strands flat and tight as you plait.

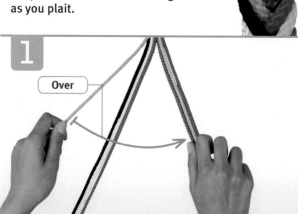

1

Over

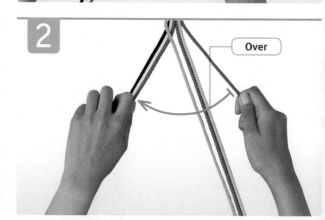

2

Over

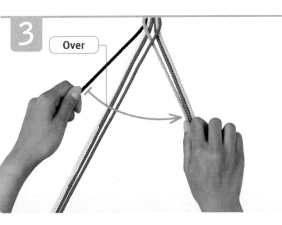

3

Over

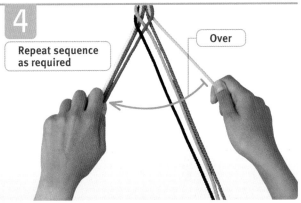

4

Repeat sequence as required

Over

5 **WHIP (»pp.374–75) STRANDS TOGETHER TO FINISH**

BEST FOR ...
Gifts

There are a number of knots that are decorative as well as practical. They are ideal for making attractive and useful gifts.

Monkey's Fist » pp.49–53

✓ A decorative ball knot that is perfect for making a key fob. Seize (*see pp.387–89*) a loop on the end to attach the keys.

✓ Can also be turned into a doorstop – simply tie the knot with large rope, and place a weight in its centre.

Similar knots:
**» pp.62–71
Manrope Knot**

Basic Net » pp.283–84

✓ Used to make a durable, lasting net.

✓ The finished net can be as large or small as you want, and may be used for storage or even as part of a hammock.

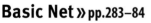

Similar knots:
**» pp.285–86
Cargo Net Knot**

✗ Requires the use of a netting needle (*see p.19*).

True Lover's Knot
» pp.80–81

✓ One of many knots used as as a symbol of binding love between two people.

✓ Can be mounted in a frame to make a wedding present.

✓ The two Overhand Knots (*see pp.28–29*) are separate but interlinked.

Similar knots:
» pp.82–84
Sailor's Cross

Square Crown Sennit » pp.330–31

✓ Easily made into a bracelet or belt.

✓ Highly decorative, but relatively simple to make.

✓ A core can be added to the centre of the sennit to create a key fob.

Similar knots:
» pp.327–29
Six-Strand
Round Crowning

Turk's Head – Four-Lead Five-Bight
» pp.128–32

✓ Can be used to make a decorative napkin ring.

✓ Can also be flattened to make a small mat or coaster.

✓ The knot's structure can be stiffened by covering the inside of it with PVA glue.

Similar knots:
» pp.117–23
Turk's Head –
Three-Lead
Four-Bight

Oval Mat » pp.311–15

✓ Can be used to make a coaster, table mat, or doormat.

✓ Thinner rope is best for a coaster or table mat, thicker rope for a doormat.

✓ The pattern can be doubled or tripled, as required.

Similar knots:
» pp.306–10
Ocean-Plait Mat

Ocean-Plait Mat

- Used to make a decorative mat.
- Tie loosely before working into a neat, taut final shape.
- Follow the pattern around two, three, four, or even five times to make a larger mat.

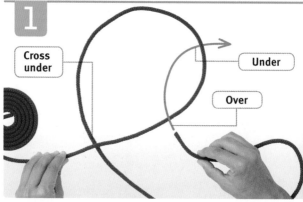

Cross under | **Under** | **Over**

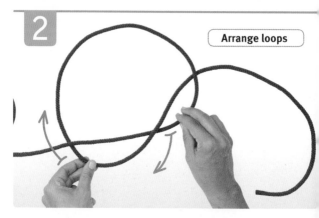

Arrange loops

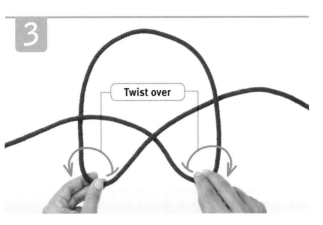

3

Twist over

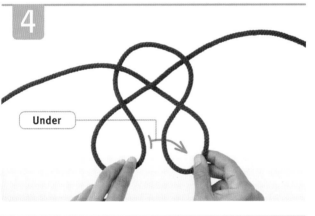

4

Under

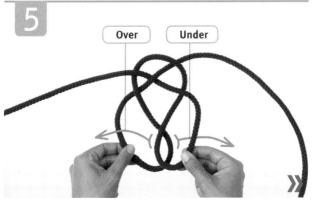

5

Over   Under

6 Make crossed strands even

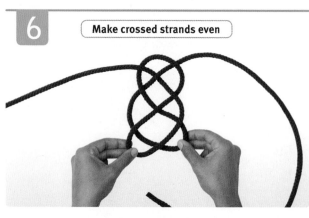

7

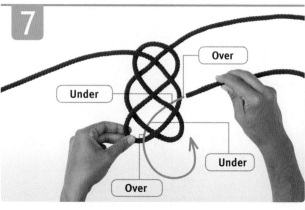

Over

Under

Under

Over

8 Make crossed strands even

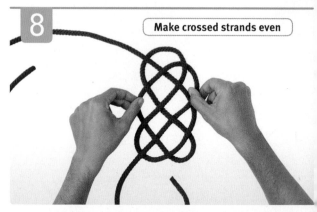

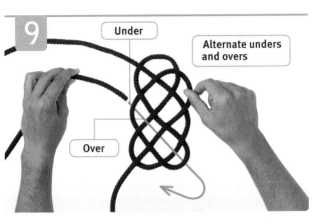

9

Under

Alternate unders and overs

Over

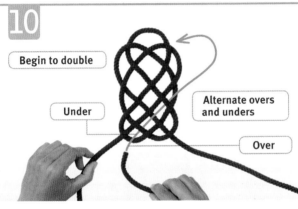

10

Begin to double

Under

Alternate overs and unders

Over

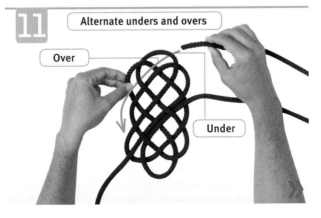

11

Alternate unders and overs

Over

Under

12

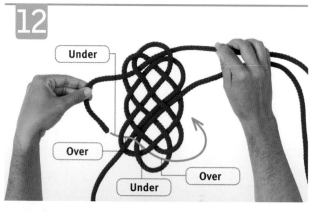

Under

Over

Under

Over

13

Alternate unders and overs

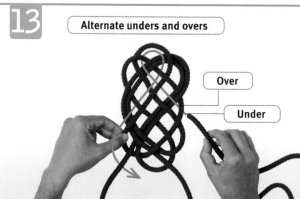

Over

Under

14

Follow around again or trim and tuck to finish

Oval Mat

- Used to make a decorative mat.
- Use thin rope for a table mat and thick rope for a doormat.
- Pattern can be followed around three or more times.
- Requires a large amount of rope.

1

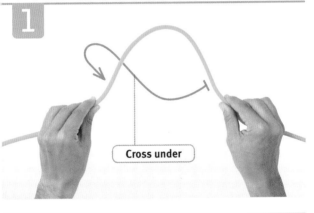

Cross under

2

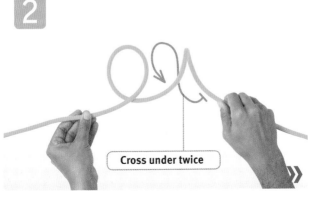

Cross under twice

»

3

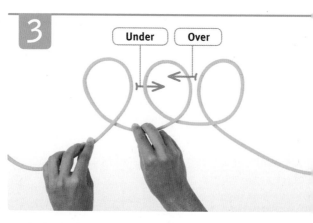

Under | Over

4

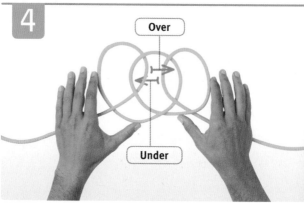

Over

Under

5

Arrange crossing turns

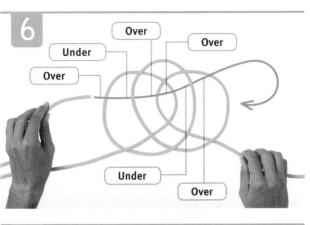

6

Over
Over
Under
Over
Under
Over

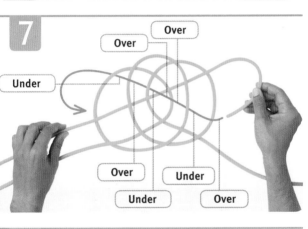

7

Over
Over
Under
Over
Under
Under
Over

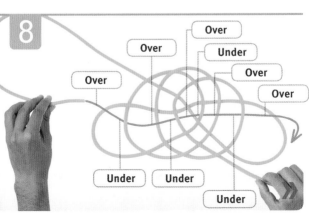

8

Over
Over
Under
Over
Over
Over
Under
Under
Under

9

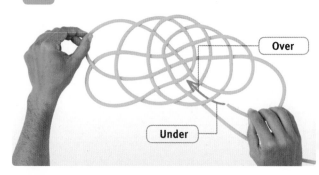

Over

Under

10

Start to double with long end, alternating overs and unders

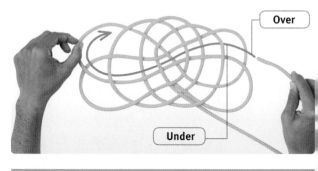

Over

Under

11

Under

Over

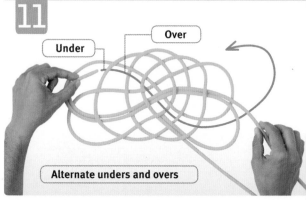

Alternate unders and overs

12

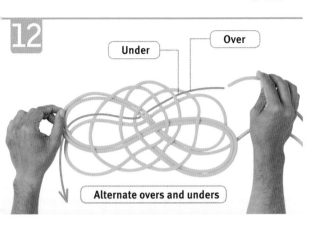

Under

Over

Alternate overs and unders

13

Alternate overs and unders

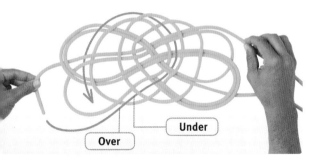

Over

Under

14

Follow around again or trim and tuck to finish

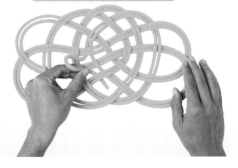

Chain Sennit

- Forms interlinked loops to shorten a rope.
- Also used by climbers to prevent rope from getting tangled.
- Work tight before moving on to the next step.
- Also known as the Drummer's Plait.

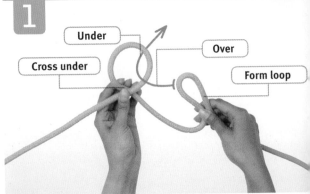

Under

Over

Cross under

Form loop

Pull

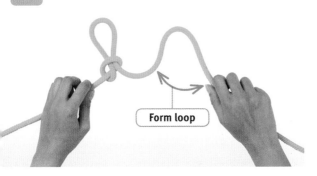

3

Form loop

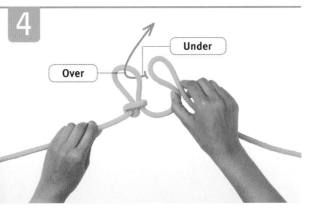

4

Over

Under

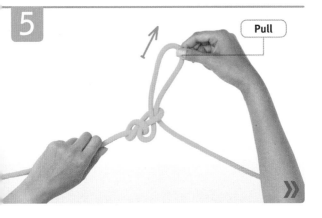

5

Pull

6

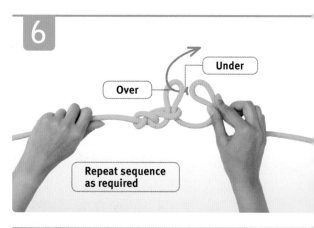

Over

Under

Repeat sequence as required

7

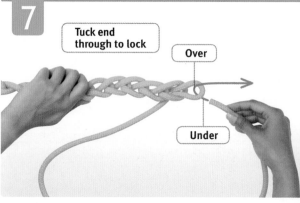

Tuck end through to lock

Over

Under

8

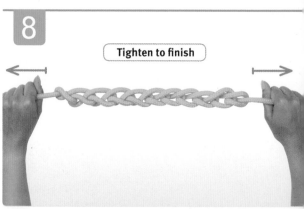

Tighten to finish

Four-Strand Round Sennit

- The simplest of the round plaits.
- Bind one end of the strands together (*see pp.374–75*) before starting.
- Keep all the strands tight as you plait.
- Ensure that you untangle the working ends regularly.

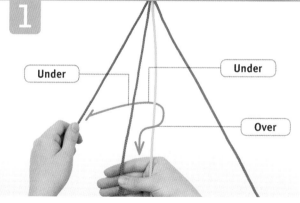

1

Under

Under

Over

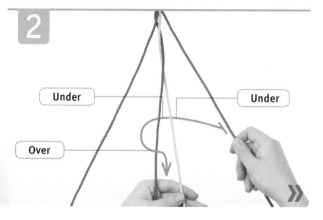

2

Under

Under

Over

3

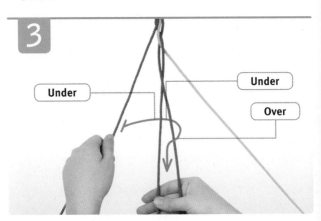

Under

Under

Over

4

Repeat sequence as required

Under

Under

Over

5

WHIP (≫pp.374–75) STRANDS TOGETHER TO FINISH

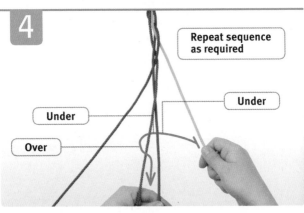

Eight-Strand Square Sennit

- A highly decorative sennit.
- Bind one end of the strands together (*see pp.374–75*) before starting.
- Move alternate outer strands to the middle of the plait.
- If you stop while tying, ensure that you start at the correct point in the sequence.

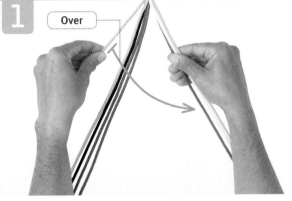

1 Over

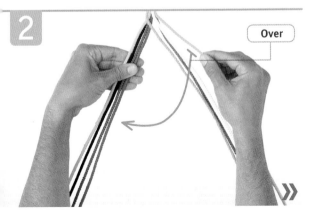

2 Over

»

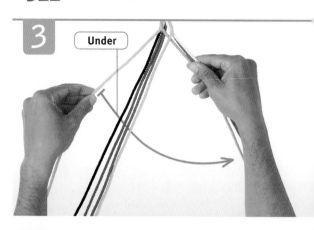

3 | Under

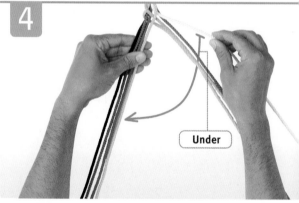

4 | Under

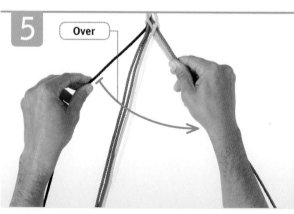

5 | Over

6

Over

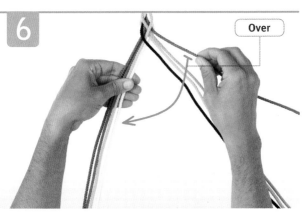

7

Under

Repeat sequence
as required

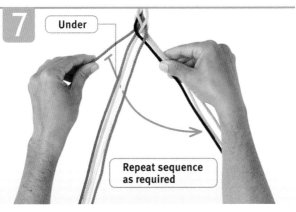

8 WHIP (»pp.374–75) STRANDS TOGETHER TO FINISH

Round Crown Sennit

- Used to convert lengths of line into an attractive, solid braid.
- Formed from a series of Crown Knots (see pp.54–55) tied one on top of another.
- Bind one end of the strands together (see pp.374–75) before starting.

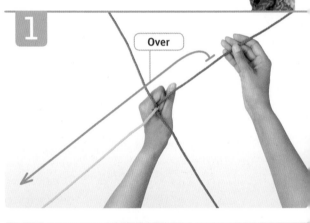

1

Over

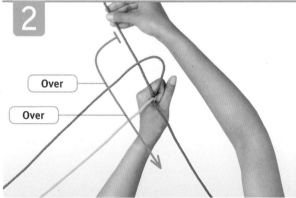

2

Over

Over

3

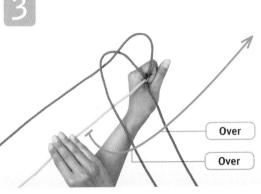

Over

Over

4

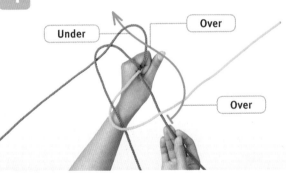

Under

Over

Over

5

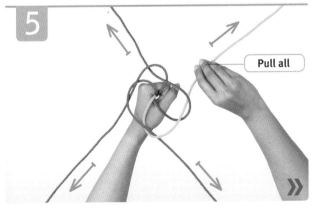

Pull all

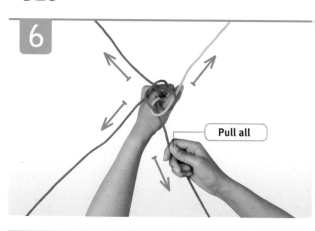

6

Pull all

7

Repeat sequence
as required

Round Crown Sennit – Four Pairs

- Uses pairs of line instead
  of single strands to make a
  bulkier sennit.
- Follows the same pattern
  as the Round Crown Sennit
  (*see pp.324–26*).

Six-Strand Round Crowning

- Used to form a cylindrical tube from a sennit.
- Made by tying a series of Crown Knots (see pp.54–55).
- Bind one end of the strands together (see pp.374–75) before starting.
- Not suitable for use in large-diameter rope.

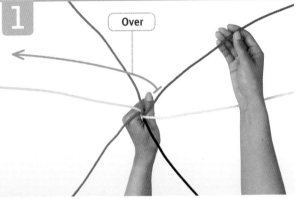

1

Over

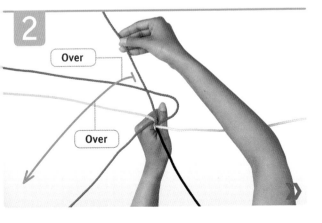

2

Over

Over

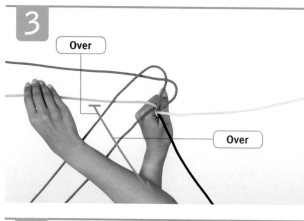

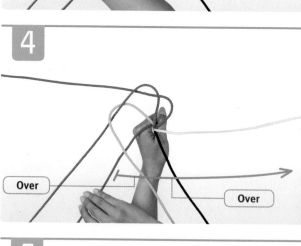

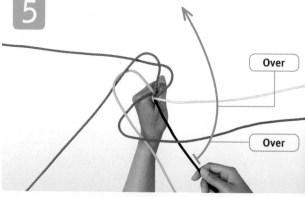

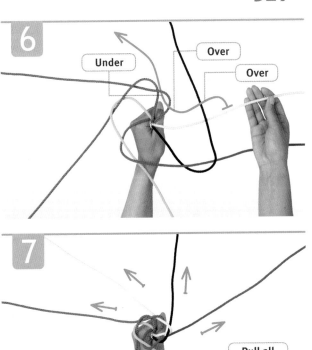

Under
Over
Over

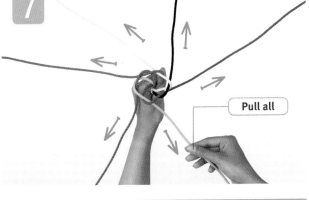

Pull all

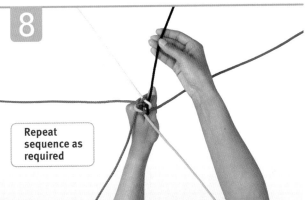

Repeat
sequence as
required

Square Crown Sennit

- A decorative knot used in cords and bracelets.
- Formed from Crown Knots (see pp.54–55) tied in alternate directions.
- Bind one end of the strands together (see pp.374–75) before starting.
- Tighten each Crown Knot before moving to the next stage.

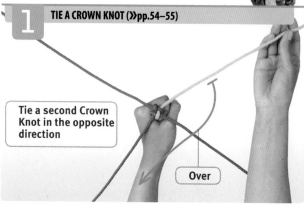

1 TIE A CROWN KNOT (»pp.54–55)

Tie a second Crown Knot in the opposite direction

Over

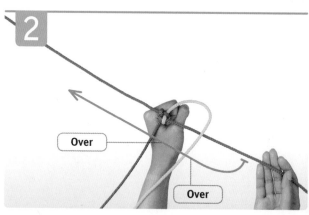

2

Over

Over

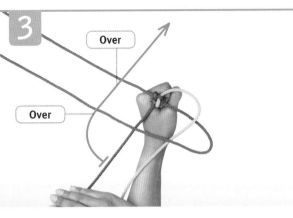

3

Over

Over

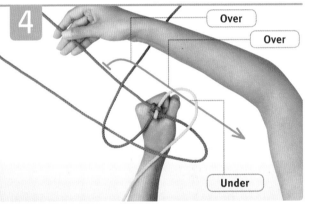

4

Over

Over

Under

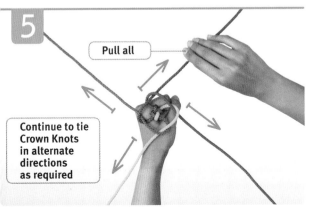

5

Pull all

Continue to tie
Crown Knots
in alternate
directions
as required

Splices and Whippings

A splice is a permanent way of finishing a rope using its strands or of joining together two ropes of equal width. A whipping is tied at the end of a rope and prevents it from coming undone.

Back Splice

- Used as a permanent finish to the end of a rope.
- Increases the diameter of a rope end by one-third.
- Before you start tie a Crown Knot (*see pp.54–55*) with the strands, leaving long strand ends.
- Whip (*see pp.374–75*) or tape the working ends to make the strands easier to tuck.

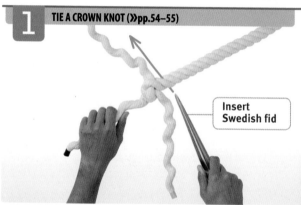

1 TIE A CROWN KNOT (»pp.54–55)

Insert Swedish fid

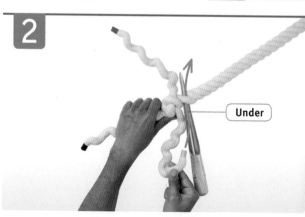

2

Under

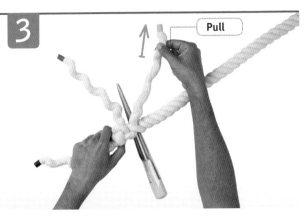

3

Pull

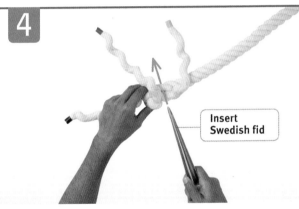

4

Insert
Swedish fid

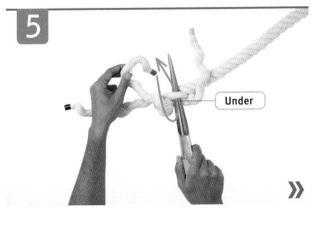

5

Under

»

6

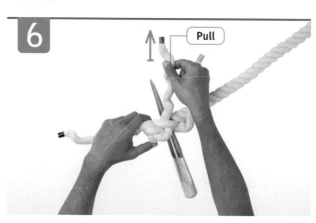

Pull

7

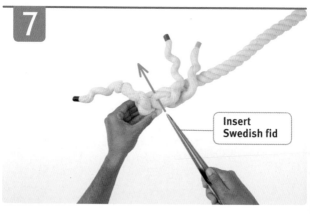

Insert
Swedish fid

8

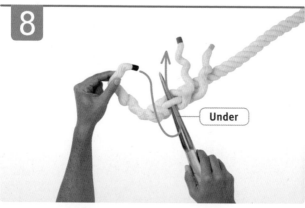

Under

9

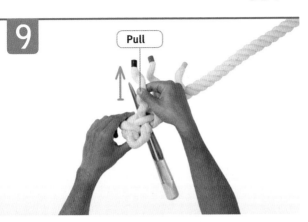

Pull

10

Arrange strands

11

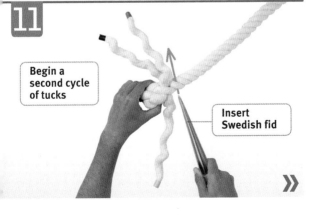

Begin a second cycle of tucks

Insert Swedish fid

»

12

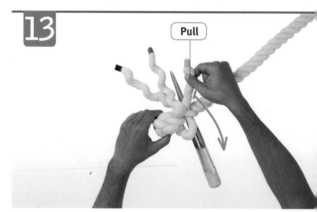

Under

13

Pull

14

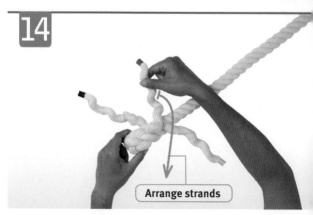

Arrange strands

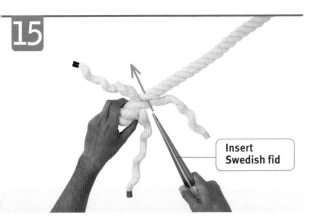

15

Insert
Swedish fid

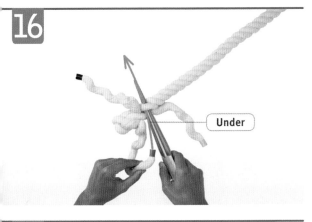

16

Under

17

Pull

»

18

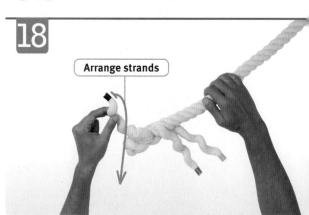

Arrange strands

19

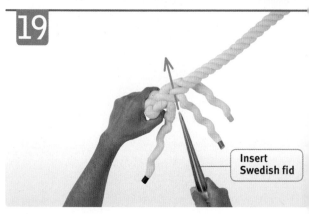

Insert Swedish fid

20

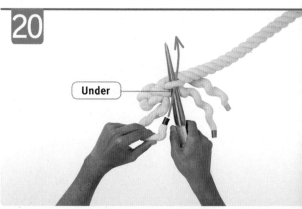

Under

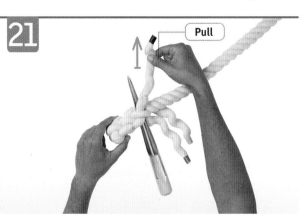

21

Pull

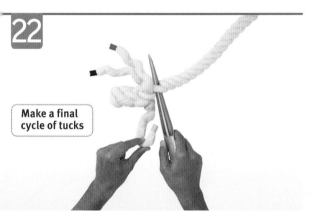

22

Make a final
cycle of tucks

23

Trim to finish

Eye Splice

- Forms a permanent loop at the end of a three-strand rope.
- Ensure a tight start to the splice.
- Make a minimum of three full tucks for a natural fibre rope and five tucks for synthetic rope, as it is more slippery.

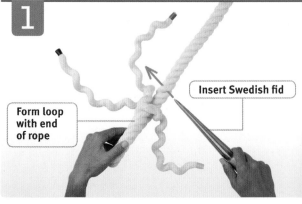

1

Form loop with end of rope

Insert Swedish fid

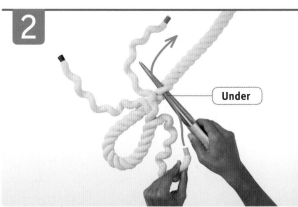

2

Under

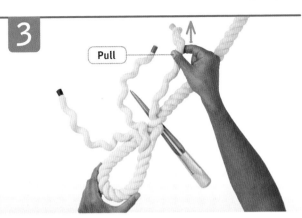

3

Pull

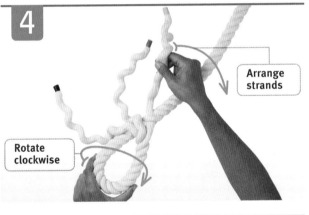

4

Arrange strands

Rotate clockwise

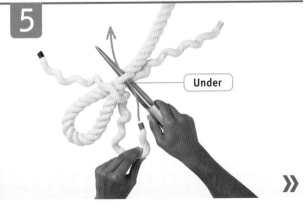

5

Under

»

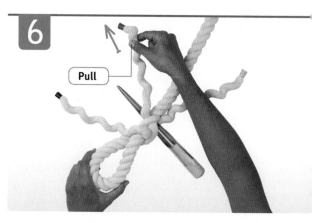

6

Pull

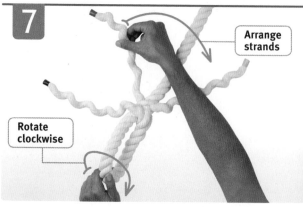

7

Arrange strands

Rotate clockwise

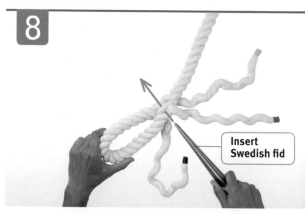

8

Insert Swedish fid

9

Under

10

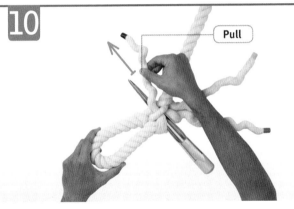

Pull

11

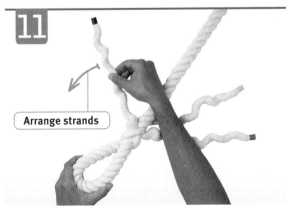

Arrange strands

»

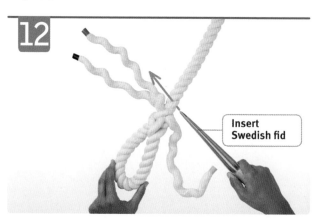

12

Insert
Swedish fid

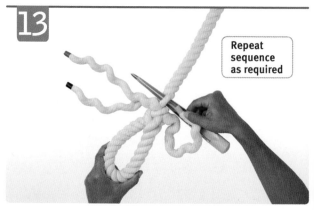

13

Repeat
sequence
as required

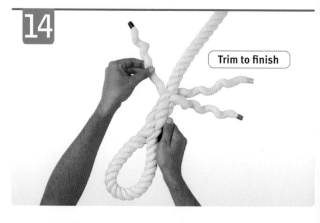

14

Trim to finish

Short Splice

- A method for permanently joining two ropes of equal thickness.
- Produces a thicker rope.
- May be tapered (*see pp.364–69*) if desired.
- Use a fid or Swedish fid (*see p.19*) to make it easier to separate the strands.
- Make three cycles of tucks each way for natural rope and five for synthetic.

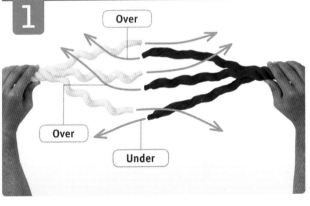

1

Over

Over

Under

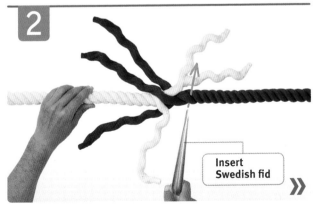

2

Insert
Swedish fid

》

3

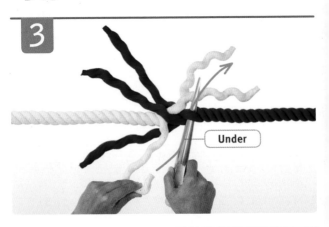

Under

4

Pull

Remove
Swedish fid

5

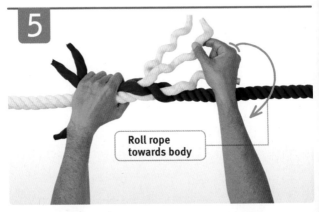

Roll rope
towards body

6

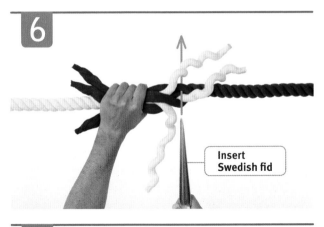

Insert
Swedish fid

7

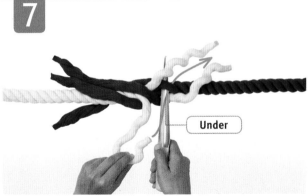

Under

8

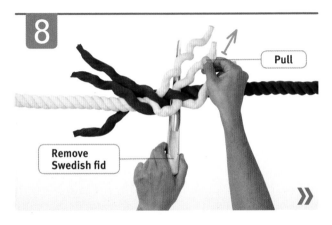

Pull

Remove
Swedish fid

»

9

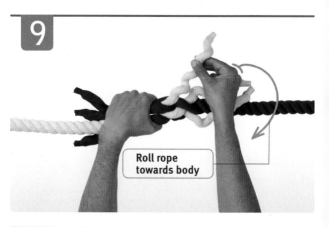

Roll rope towards body

10

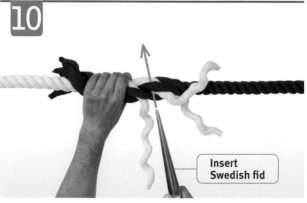

Insert Swedish fid

11

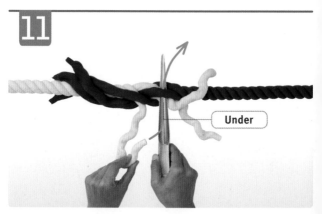

Under

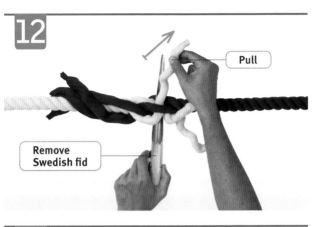

12

Pull

Remove Swedish fid

13

Roll rope towards body

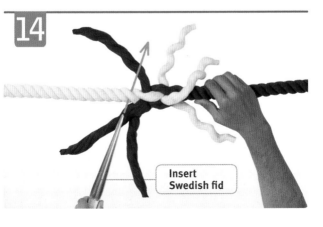

14

Insert Swedish fid

15

Under

16

Pull

Remove
Swedish fid

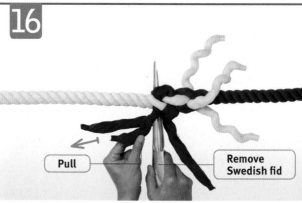

17

Roll rope
towards
body

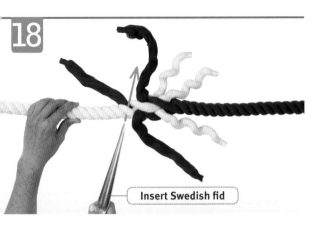

18

Insert Swedish fid

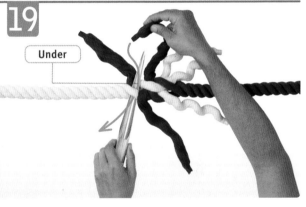

19

Under

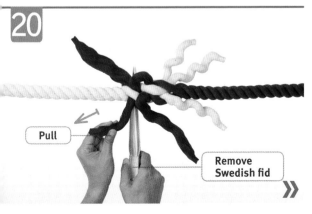

20

Pull

Remove
Swedish fid

»

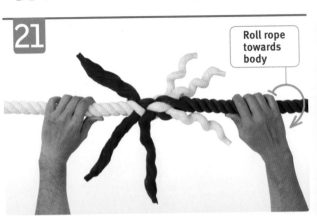

21 Roll rope towards body

22 Insert Swedish fid

23 Under

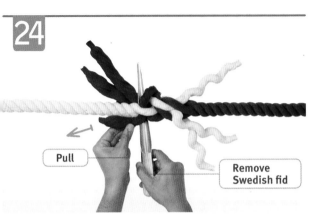

24

Pull

Remove
Swedish fid

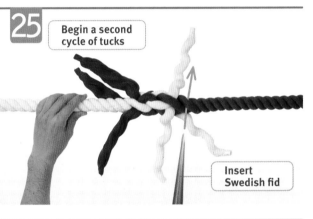

25

Begin a second
cycle of tucks

Insert
Swedish fid

26

Under

》

27

Pull

Remove
Swedish fid

28

Roll rope
towards body

29

Insert
Swedish fid

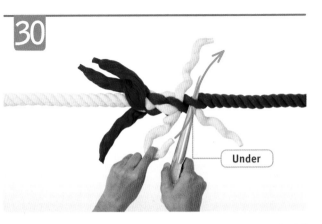

30

Under

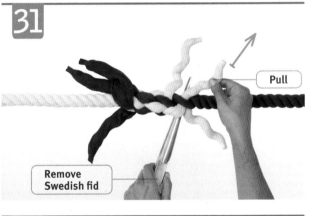

31

Pull

Remove
Swedish fid

32

Roll rope
towards body

33

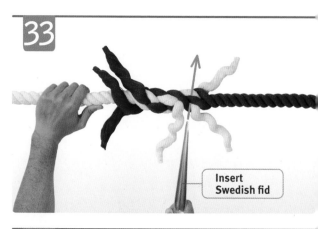

Insert
Swedish fid

34

Under

35

Pull

Remove
Swedish fid

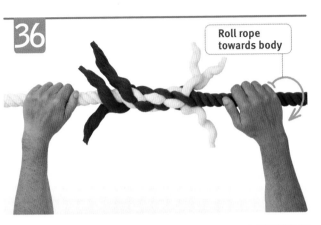

36

Roll rope towards body

37

Begin a third cycle of tucks

Insert Swedish fid

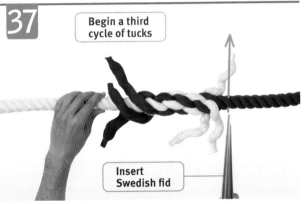

38

Under

»

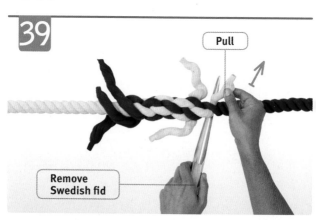

39

Pull

Remove
Swedish fid

40

Roll rope away
from body

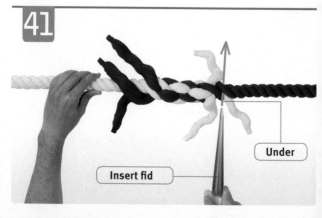

41

Under

Insert fid

42

Under

43

Pull

44

Roll rope away from body

45

Insert
Swedish fid

46

Under

47

Pull

Remove
Swedish fid

48

Roll rope away from body

49

Repeat second and third cycle of tucks on the opposite side of the splice

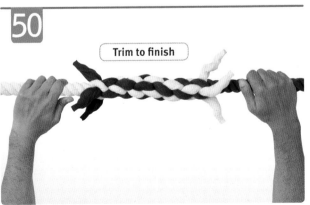

50

Trim to finish

Tapering a Splice

- Used to taper the ends of a spliced (*see pp.334–63*) three-strand rope to prevent it from working loose.
- Can be used to strengthen and neaten all splices.

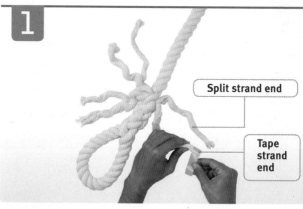

1

Split strand end

Tape strand end

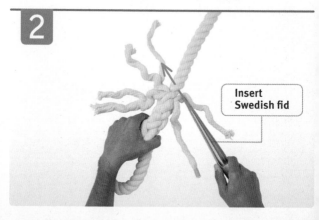

2

Insert Swedish fid

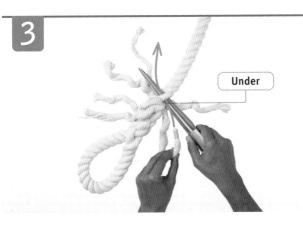

3

Under

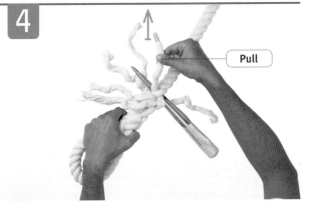

4

Pull

5

Arrange
strands

»

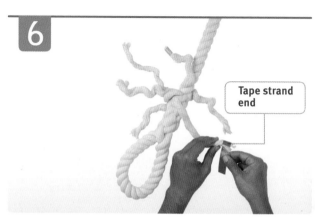

6

Tape strand end

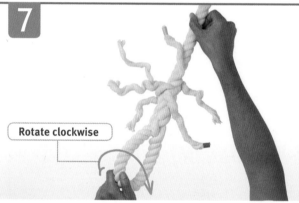

7

Rotate clockwise

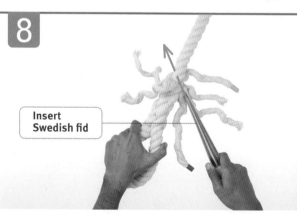

8

Insert Swedish fid

9

Under

10

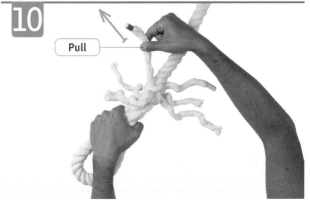

Pull

11

Arrange
strands

»

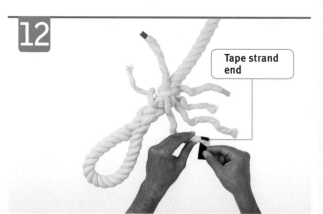

Tape strand end

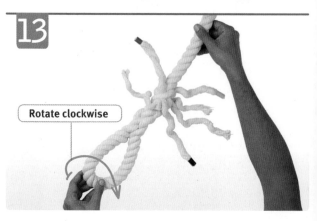

Rotate clockwise

Insert Swedish fid

15

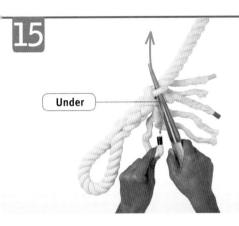

Under

16

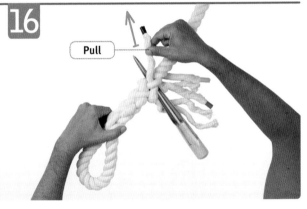

Pull

17

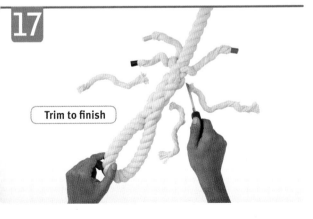

Trim to finish

BEST FOR ...
Horses

Equestrians use knots for a multitude of reasons such as tethering horses safely, fixing clips, tying straps and webbing, and securing ropes around a horse's neck or on the horn of a saddle.

Eye Splice
》 pp.342–46

✅ Offers a neat and reliable method for making an eye through which to attach clips to lead ropes.

✅ Should be formed at the end of ropes that are used for pulling, dragging, or hoisting.

✅ Can also be used to make a halter.

Similar knots:
》 pp.334–41
Back Splice

Back Splice 》 p.334–41

✅ Also known as an End Splice, this is a permanent fastening that stops the end of a rope from coming undone.

✅ Can also be used to make a grip at the end of a rope.

Similar knots:
》 pp.342–46
Eye Splice

Round Turn and Two Half Hitches » pp.180–81

✅ A quick, safe method for tying up a horse – the round turn means it can handle a large amount of strain.

✅ A reasonably easy hitch to untie, even if a large amount of strain has been placed on it.

Similar knots:
**» pp.182–83
Buntline Hitch
» pp.184–85
Fisherman's Bend**

Water Knot » pp.172–73

✅ An effective method for linking flat strapping and webbing of the type found on a horse's bridle.

✅ Can also be used to make an emergency repair to broken reins.

✅ A knot that is both strong and reliable.

Similar knots:
**» pp.157–59
Fisherman's Knot**

Highwayman's Hitch » pp.201–02

✓ A quick-release hitch that is good for temporarily tethering a horse to a ring or rail.

✗ Comes undone easily, so the hitch must always be pulled tight, with a good locking bight, before leaving the horse.

Similar knots:
» pp.180–81
Round Turn and Two Half Hitches

Three-Strand Flat Plait » pp.292–93

✓ Simple and quick to tie, this plait can be made as long as desired.

✓ When secured with a rubber plaiting band it can be used to dress a horse's mane or tail.

✓ A ribbon, held in place with a plaiting band, can be added for extra decoration.

Similar knots:
» pp.294–95 Four-Strand Flat Plait
» pp.296–97 Five-Strand Flat Plait

Common Whipping

- Prevents the end of a rope from fraying.
- The simplest of all whippings.
- Waxing the twine makes it easier to pull the loop under the whipping turns.
- To finish, use a Marlinespike Hitch (*see pp.199–200*) to prevent fine twine from cutting your fingers.

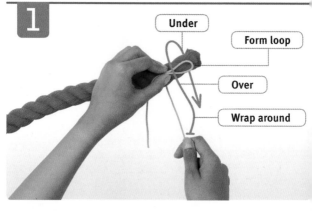

1

Under

Form loop

Over

Wrap around

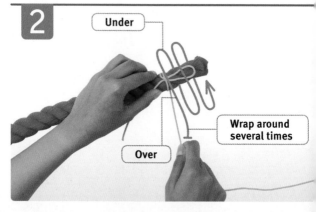

2

Under

Wrap around several times

Over

3

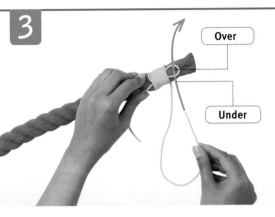

Over

Under

4

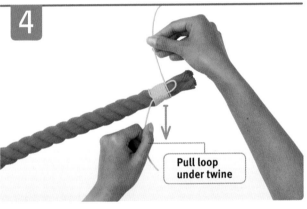

Pull loop under twine

5

Tighten and trim to finish

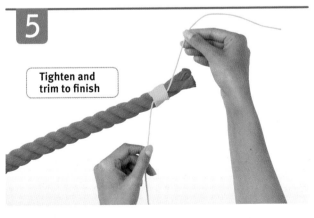

French Whipping

- A decorative whipping used to stop a rope end from unravelling.
- Also used over railings or tool handles to provide a firm grip.
- Formed using a series of half hitches (*see p.23*) tied in the same direction.
- Secure the twine around the rope with an Overhand Knot (*see pp.28–29*) before starting.

1 SECURE TWINE WITH AN OVERHAND KNOT (»pp.28–29)

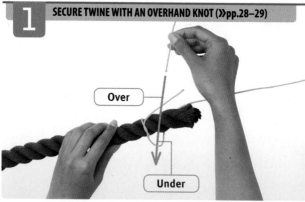

Over

Under

2

Tie a half hitch around the rope

Under

3

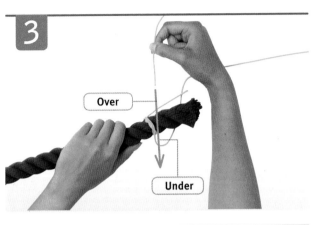

Over

Under

4

Make several more half hitches

Over

Under

Under

Under

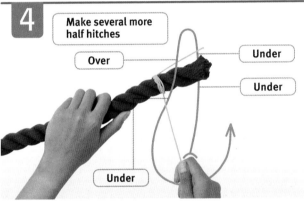

5

Under

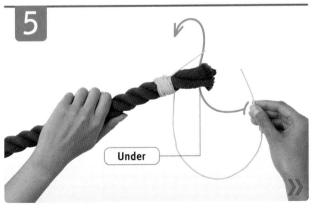

6

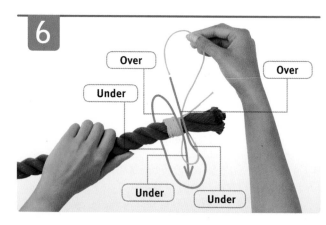

Over

Under

Over

Under

Under

7

Pull

8

Tighten and trim to finish

Sailmaker's Whipping

- The most secure finish for the end of a three-strand rope.
- Can only be made at the end of the rope.
- Whipping should be roughly one-and-a-half times the diameter of the rope.

1

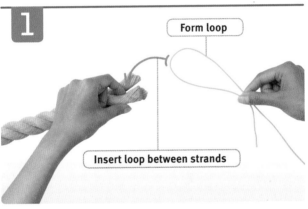

Form loop

Insert loop between strands

2

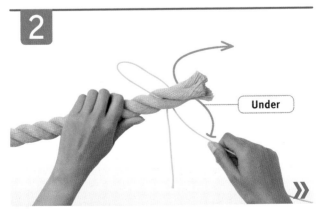

Under

3

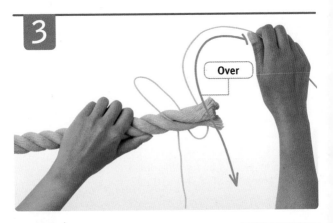

Over

4

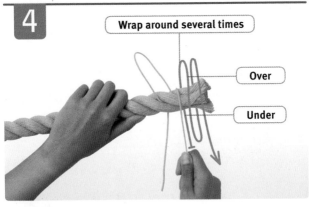

Wrap around several times

Over

Under

5

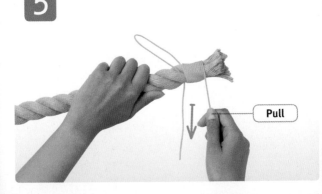

Pull

6

Insert loop between strands

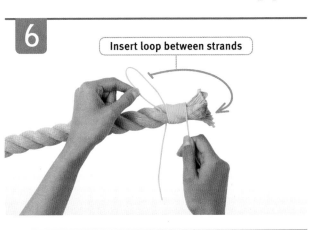

7

Pull

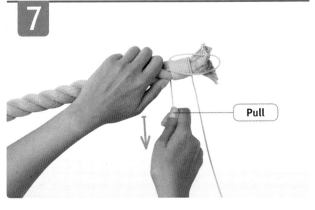

8

Pull to tighten

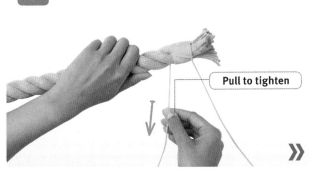

»

9

Insert twine between strands

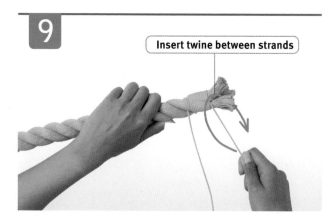

10

Over

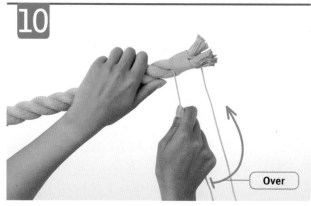

11 FINISH WITH A REEF KNOT (»pp.85–86)

Palm and Needle Whipping

- The perfect whipping to secure a braided rope.
- Can be used in the middle of a rope.
- Requires a palm and a sailmaker's needle (*see p.19*).
- Preferred by sailmakers.

1

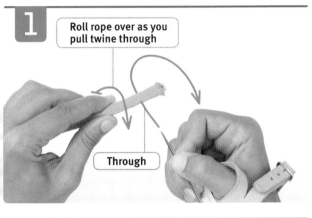

Roll rope over as you pull twine through

Through

2

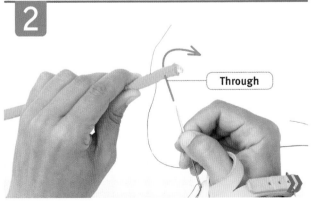

Through

3

Roll rope towards body

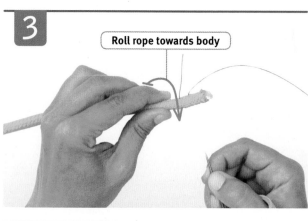

4

Hold thread with thumb

Through

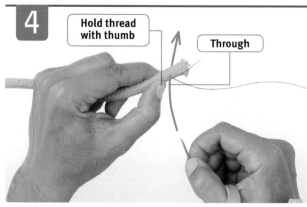

5

Wrap around to cover stitches

Under

Over

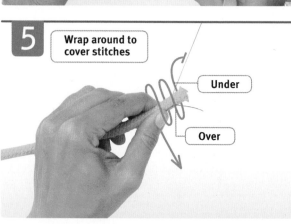

6

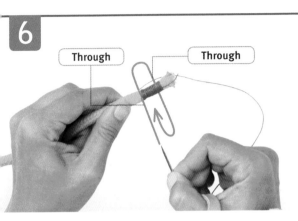

Through

Through

7

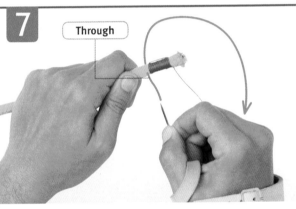

Through

8

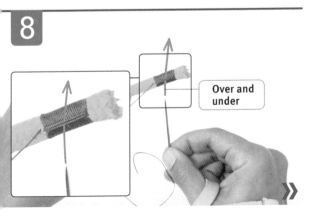

Over and under

9

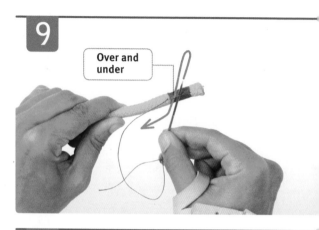

Over and under

10

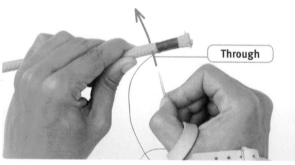

Through

11

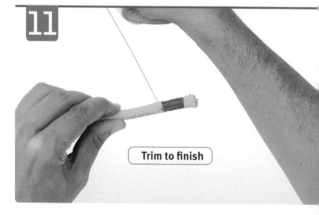

Trim to finish

Seizing

- A tightly compressed whipping that can be used to bind two parts of a rope together.
- Historically used on the heavy fixed rigging found on sailing ships.
- Must be tied tightly and evenly.

1 **SECURE TWINE WITH A CONSTRICTOR KNOT (»pp.109–10)**

Over

Wrap around

Form loop

Under

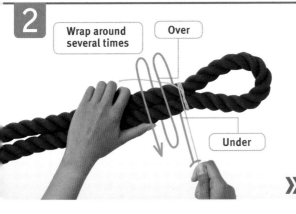

2

Wrap around several times

Over

Under

»

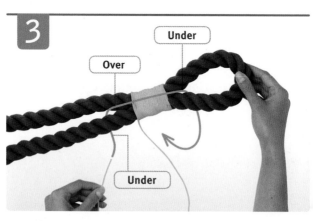

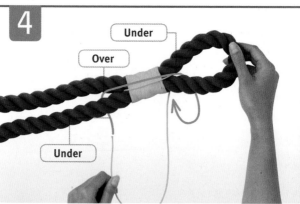

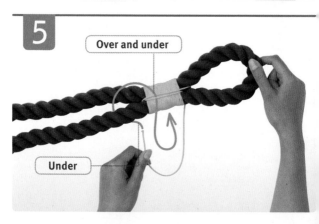

6

Under and over

Over

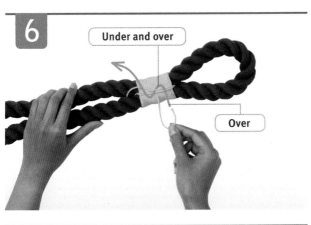

7

Pull to secure

8

Tighten and trim to finish

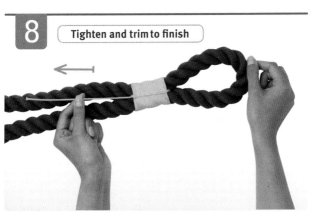

Stitch and Seize

- Used to make a permanent eye on the end of a braided rope.
- Requires a palm and a sailmaker's needle (*see p.19*).
- Stitch first, then seize over the stitches.
- Make a locking stitch along the seizing halfway through the process for additional security.

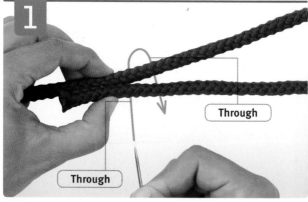

1

Through

Through

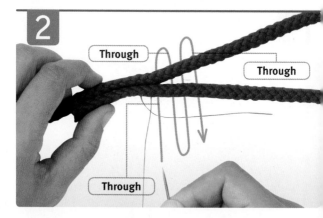

2

Through

Through

Through

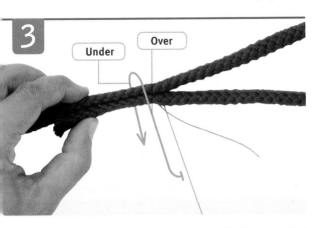

Under Over

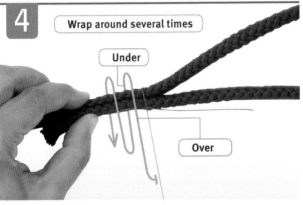

Wrap around several times

Under

Over

Through

»

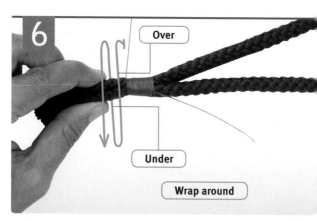

6

Over

Under

Wrap around

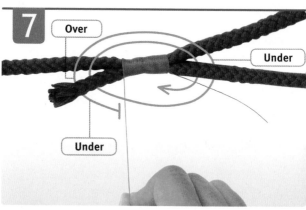

7

Over

Under

Under

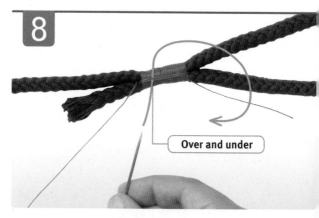

8

Over and under

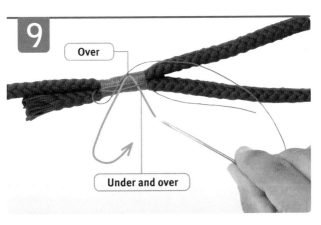

9

Over

Under and over

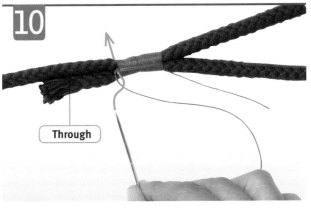

10

Through

11

Trim to finish

Glossary

As well as explaining the knotting terms used in this book, this glossary also features some specialized climbing and sailing terms.

Belay To secure one climber to another with a rope.

Bight 1 The part of a rope that is folded back on itself to form a narrow loop. **2** The curved side of a knot.

Blood knot Knot consisting of many turns, used in angling or climbing.

Boat hook In sailing, a pole with a hook on one end, used to help catch hold of a rope or ring.

Body The tied part of a knot.

Braid Strands or yarns woven or plaited together in a regular pattern.

Braided rope Rope consisting of multiple woven or plaited strands or yarns.

Breaking rope The part of a rope that controls the amount of slip of a knot, and that restricts the amount of slip a knot has during a fall.

Chafe The frayed part of a rope, caused by abrasion against a rough surface.

Cleat On a boat, a fitting around which a rope is wound to secure it.

Coil A rope that has been placed into a neat series of circles or loops, often for storage purposes.

Cordage The general term for rope.

Core The inner part of a rope which is made from parallel, twisted, or braided rope fibres.

Crossing turn A circle of rope made by crossing one end of a rope over itself.

Eve 1 A hole in a knot. **2** The hole inside a circle of rope. **3** A permanent loop fabricated at the end of a piece of rope. **4** The opening at the end of a fishing hook, through which a line can be threaded.

Fid A sharp, pointed wooden tool used to separate strands of rope.

Frapping turns Extra turns made across lashing, whipping, or seizing turns.

Half hitch A circle of rope wound around an object or boat fitting. It is kept in place by placing one end of the rope across and at right angles to the other end.

Hard-laid rope Tightly twisted, three-strand rope designed to be very stiff and firm.

Heaving line The light line attached to a mooring rope that is thrown from a boat and used to haul a mooring rope ashore.

Karabiner In climbing, a D-shaped or oval metal snaplink fitted with a locking device.

Laid rope A rope made by twisting strands of yarn together.

Large-diameter rope Rope of around 24mm diameter or more.

Lash; lashing To secure two or more adjacent or crossed poles by binding them with rope; the term for the binding itself.

Lashing turn A turn used to bind poles together, as part of a lashing.

Lay The direction in which the twists of the strands in a laid rope lie.

Lead The number of strands used to make a plait, used particularly in a Turk's Head knot.

Line A length of rope measuring less than 4mm in diameter.

Loaded rope The part of a rope that applies force to a climbing knot.

Loop A circle of rope made by placing two parts of a rope together, without crossing them over.

Marlinsepike A slim, pointed, metal spike that is commonly used to separate strands of rope.

Netting needle A pointed tool used for manipulating fine line when making a net.

Palm A glovelike, leather strap containing a metal plate and worn on the hand, to protect the palm while pushing a sailmaker's needle through a rope.

Rigger Ships' rigging manufacturer.

Rigging Ropes and spars designed to control the sails of a ship.

Round turn A complete circle, followed by a half circle, made with a length of rope around an object.

Seize; seizing The process of joining two ropes, or two lengths of a rope, by binding them with twine; the term for the binding itself.

Sheath A covering made from woven strands intended to protect the core of a rope.

Sheet Rope that controls a sail.

Shock cord Rope with a high degree of stretch, made from a rubber elastic core covered by a braided protective sheath of nylon fibres, also known as elasticated cord.

Sling A continuous circle made from rope or tape that can be made by tying the ends of the material with a Fisherman's Knot or a Water Knot. Also referred to as a strop.

Small-diameter rope Rope with a diameter of approximately 4–8mm.

Spade end The flat end of a hook, with no eye for threading line.

Standing part The length of a rope not used or in reserve during the tying of a knot.

Swedish fid A hollow, pointed, metal-bladed tool for tucking strand ends when splicing stiff rope.

Tape In climbing, the flat, woven webbing used to make slings.

Thin line A piece of line measuring less than 2mm in diameter.

Three-strand rope Rope consisting of three strands twisted together.

Tuck To pass one part of a rope underneath another part of itself.

Turn To pass a rope around one side of an object.

Unlaid rope A rope separated into its component strands.

Whipping turn The turn made around the end of a length of rope, as part of a whipping.

Whipping twine A type of thin line, sometimes made from nylon, that is used to bind the end of a rope.

Working end When tying a knot, the end of a rope used.

Working load The maximum load to which a rope should be subjected.

Yarn Natural or synthetic fibres twisted into threads.

Index

A

A-Frame Lashing 224
Alpine Butterfly 167, **238–39**
Angler's Loop **267–68**
Ashley's Bend **155–56**

B

Bachmann Knot **230–31**
Back Splice **334–41**, 371
Barrel Knot *see* Blood Knot
Basic Net **283–84**, 303
bends
  Ashley's Bend **155–56**
  Barrel Knot *see* Blood Knot
  Blood Knot **168–71**, 275
  Carrick Bend **148–49**
  Double Fisherman's Knot **160–63**, 166
  Double Overhand Bend *see* Water Knot
  Double Sheet Bend 36, 140, **144–45**, 221
  Fisherman's Knot **157–59**, 271
  Friendship Knot *see* Lanyard Knot
  Hunter's Bend **150–51**
  Lanyard Knot **152–54**
  Rigger's Bend *see* Hunter's Bend
  Rope Yarn Knot **146–47**
  Sheet Bend 36, **140–41**, 221, 283
  Tucked Sheet Bend 36, **142–43**

bends (cont.)
  Water Knot **172–73**, 372
Bimini Twist 277, **280–82**
binding knots
  Boa Knot **114–16**
  Clove Hitch **105–06**, 211, 222, 303
  Clove Hitch, Second Method **107–08**
  Constrictor Knot 14, **109–10**, 114, 126, 219
  Granny Knot **92–93**
  Packer's Knot **102–04**, 127
  Reef Knot *see* Reef Knot
  Sailor's Cross **82–84**, 304
  Square Knot *see* Reef Knot
  Surgeon's Knot *see* Surgeon's Knot
  Thief Knot **94–95**
  Timber Hitch **111–13**, 221
  True Lover's Knot **80–81**, 82, 304
  Turk's Head *see* Turk's Head
  Turquoise Turtle **99–101**, 126
Blood Dropper Knot 277, **278–79**
Blood Knot **168–71**, 275
Boa Knot **114–16**
Bowline 35, 189, **240–41**, 251
  on the Bight **259–61**
  Portuguese **262–64**
  Second Method 35, **242–44**
  Spanish **265–66**
  with Stopper 35, 167, **248**
  with Two Turns 35, **245–47**

Buntline Hitch **182–83**
Butcher's Knot *see* Packer's Knot

C

camping 186–89
Cargo Net Knot **285–86**, 303
Carrick Bend **148–49**
Chain Sennit **316–18**
climbing 11, 13, 164–67
  Alpine Butterfly 167, **238–39**
  Bachmann Knot **230–31**
  Bowline *see* Bowline
  Chain Sennit **316–18**
  Double Fisherman's Knot **160–63**, 166
  Figure of Eight *see* Figure of Eight
  Fisherman's Knot **157–59**, 271
  Italian Hitch 165, **234–35**
  Klemheist Knot **232–33**
  Prusik Knot 165, **228–29**, 232
  Reversed Italian Hitch **235**
  Water Knot **172–73**, 372
Clinch Knot **207–08**
Clove Hitch **105–06**, 211, 222, 303
  Second Method **107–08**
Common Whipping **374–75**
Constrictor Knot 14, **109–10**, 114, 126, 219
Cow Hitch **190–91**, 303
  Pedigree **191**
  Second Method **107–08**
  with Toggle **192–93**
Crown Knot **54–55**, 334

D

decorative knotting
10, 12
Boa Knot **114–16**
French Whipping
376–78
gifts 302–05
see also decorative
knots
Lanyard Knot
152–54
Monkey's Fist **49–53**,
303
Sailor's Cross **82–84**,
304
Stopper Knot
42–43
Turk's Head see
Turk's Head
Turquoise Turtle
99–101, 126
see also plaits and
sennits
Diagonal Lashing
215–17
Diamond Knot **72–77**
domestic knots
124–27
Double Figure-of-Eight
Knot see
Figure-of-Eight
Loop
Double Overhand Bend
see Water Knot
Double Overhand Knot
32–33, 255
Double Overhand Loop
255–56
Double Overhand
Sliding Loop
257–58
Drummer's Plait see
Chain Sennit

E

Eight-Strand Square
Sennit **321–23**
Englishman's Loop
271–73
Double **273**
Eye Splice **342–46**,
371

F

Figure of Eight 35,
38–39, 142, 166
Loop 35, **249–50**,
276
Single Loop on the
Bight **269–70**
Slipped **40–41**
Threaded Loop
251–52
Fisherman's Bend
184–85
Fisherman's Knot
157–59, 271
Double **160–63**, 166
fishing 11, 274–77
Angler's Loop
267–68
Basic Net **283–84**,
303
Bimini Twist 277,
280–82
Blood Dropper Knot
277, **278–79**
Blood Knot **168–71**,
275
Cargo Net Knot
285–86, 303
Clinch Knot **207–08**
Figure-of-Eight Loop
35, **249–50**, 276
Overland Loop see
Overland Loop
Palomar Knot
209–10, 275
Snelling a Hook
205–06, 276
Flat Plait
Five-Strand **296–97**
Four-Strand **294–95**
Seven-Strand **300–01**
Six-Strand **298–99**
Three-Strand **292–93**
Four-Strand Round
Sennit **319–20**
French Hitching see
French Whipping
French Whipping
376–78
Friendship Knot see
Lanyard Knot

G

gardening 218–21
gifts **302–05**
see also decorative
knots
Granny Knot **92–93**
Grapevine Serving see
French Whipping

H

Highwayman's Hitch
201–02, 373
hitches
A-Frame Lashing 224
Bachmann Knot
230–31
Buntline Hitch
182–83
Clinch Knot **207–08**
Cow Hitch see
Cow Hitch
Diagonal Lashing
215–17
Fisherman's Bend
184–85
Highwayman's Hitch
201–02, 373
Icicle Hitch **225–27**
Italian Hitch 165,
234–35
Klemheist Knot
232–33
Lark's Head see
Cow Hitch
Marlinespike Hitch
199–200, 374
Palomar Knot
209–10, 275
Prusik Knot 165,
228–29, 232
Reversed Italian Hitch
235
Rolling Hitch see
Rolling Hitch
Round Turn and Two
Half Hitches 36,
125, **180–81**, 188,
220, 372
Sheepshank see
Sheepshank

hitches (cont.)
Sheer Lashing 187,
219, **222–24**
Snelling a Hook
205–06, 276
Square Lashing 188,
211–14, 220
Waggoner's Hitch
127, 189, **203–04**
horses 12, **370–73**
household knots *see*
domestic knots
Hunter's Bend **150–51**

I J K

Icicle Hitch
225–27
Italian Hitch 165,
234–35
Jury Mast Knot
287–89
Klemheist Knot
232–33

L

Lanyard Knot **152–54**
Lark's Head *see*
Cow Hitch
loops
Alpine Butterfly 167,
238–39
Angler's Loop
267–68
Basic Net **283–84**,
303
Bimini Twist 277,
280–82
Blood Dropper Knot
277, **278–89**
Bowline *see* Bowline
Cargo Net Knot
285–86, 303
Englishman's Loop
271–73
Figure-of-Eight *see*
Figure of Eight
Jury Mast Knot
287–89
Overhand Loop *see*
Overhand Loop

M

Manrope Knot 54, 56,
61–71, 125
Marlinespike Hitch
199–200, 374
Matthew Walker Knot
58–60, 72
Mirrored Rolling Hitch
37, **178–79**
Monkey's Fist **49–53**,
303

O

Ocean-Plait Mat 305,
306–10
Oval Mat 305, **311–15**
Overhand Knot **28–29**
Double **32–33**, 255
Slipped **30–31**
Overhand Loop
253–54
Double **255–56**
Double Sliding
257–58

P

Packer's Knot **102–04**,
127
Palm and Needle
Whipping **383–86**
Palomar Knot **209–10**,
275
Pedigree Cow Hitch **191**
plaits and sennits
Chain Sennit **316–18**
Drummer's Plait *see*
Chain Sennit
Eight-Strand Square
Sennit **321–23**
Flat Plait *see* Flat Plait
Four-Strand Round
Sennit **319–20**
Ocean-Plait Mat 305,
306–10
Oval Mat 305,
311–15
Round Crown Sennit
see Round Crown
Sennit

plaits and sennits
(cont.)
Six-Strand Round
Crowning 305,
327–29
Square Crown Sennit
303, 305, **330–31**
Portuguese Bowline
262–64
Prusik Knot 165,
228–29, 232

R

Reef Knot 37, **85–86**, 99
Slipped **87–89**
Slipped Doubled
90–91
Reversed Italian Hitch
235
Rigger's Bend *see*
Hunter's Bend
Rolling Hitch 37,
176–77, 187, 225
Mirrored 37, **178–79**
rope
construction 10–11
maintenance 14–15
materials 12–13
shapes 18, 20
storing 16–17
turns 18, 19
see also tying
techniques
Rope Yarn Knot **146–47**
Round Crown Sennit
303, **324–26**
Four Pairs 326
Round Turn and Two
Half Hitches 37,
125, **180–81**, 188,
220, 372

S

sailing 10, 11, 13,
34–37
Bowline *see* Bowline
Figure of Eight *see*
Figure of Eight
Fisherman's Bend
184–85

sailing (cont.)
Jury Mast Knot
287–89
Manrope Knot 54, 56,
61–71, 125
Reef Knot 37, **85–86**,
99
Rolling Hitch 37,
176–77, 187, 225
Round Turn and Two
Half Hitches 36,
125, **180–81**, 188,
220, 372
Sailmaker's Whipping
379–82
Seizing 25, **387–89**
Sheet Bend 36,
140–41, 221, 283
Sailor's Cross **82–84**,
304
Seizing 25, **387–89**
sennits see plaits and
sennits
Sheepshank **194–95**
Man o' War **196–98**
Sheer Lashing 187,
219, **222–24**
Sheet Bend 36,
140–41, 221, 283
Double 36, 140,
144–45, 221
Short Splice **347–63**
Single Figure-of-Eight
Loop on the Bight
269–70
Sink Stopper Knot
44–46
Six-Strand Round
Crowning 305,
327–29
Slipped Figure of Eight
40–41
Slipped Overhand Knot
30–31
Slipped Reef Knot
87–89
Slipped Reef Knot
Doubled **90–91**
Snelling a Hook
205–06, 276
Spanish Bowline
265–66

splices and whippings
10, 14, 17, 24, 25
Back Splice **334–41**,
371
Common Whipping
374–75
Eye Splice **342–46**,
371
French Hitching see
French Whipping
French Whipping
376–78
Grapevine Serving see
French Whipping
Palm and Needle
Whipping **383–86**
Sailmaker's Whipping
379–82
Seizing 25, **387–89**
Short Splice **347–63**
Stitch and Seize
390–93
Tapering a Splice
364–69
Square Crown Sennit
303, 305, **330–31**
Square Knot see
Reef Knot
Square Lashing 188,
211–14, 220
Stevedore Knot **47–48**
Stitch and Seize
390–93
Stopper Knot **42–43**
stopper knots
Crown Knot **54–55**,
56, 334
Diamond Knot see
Diamond Knot
Figure of Eight 35,
38–39, 166
Manrope Knot see
Manrope Knot
Matthew Walker Knot
see Matthew Walker
Knot
Monkey's Fist **49–53**,
303
Overhand Knot see
Overhand Knot
Sink Stopper Knot
44–46

stopper knots (cont.)
Slipped Figure of
Eight **40–41**
Stevedore Knot **47–48**
Stopper Knot **42–43**
Thumb Knot see
Overhand Knot
Wall Knot see
Wall Knot
Surgeon's Knot **96–98**,
99
with Second Tuck **98**

T

Tapering a Splice
364–69
Thief Knot **94–95**
Threaded Figure-of-
Eight Loop **251–52**
Thumb Knot see
Overhand Knot
Timber Hitch **111–13**,
221
tools 19
True Lover's Knot
80–81, 82, 304
Tucked Sheet Bend 36,
142–43
Turk's Head 20
Five-Lead Four Bight
133–37
Four-Lead Five Bight
128–32, 304
Three-Lead Four Bight
117–23, 304
Turquoise Turtle
99–101, 126
tying techniques
20–25
seizing 25, **387–89**
see also rope

W

Waggoner's Hitch 127,
189, **203–04**
Wall Knot **56–57**, 72
Water Knot **172–73**,
372
whippings see splices
and whippings

Acknowledgments

About the Author

Des Pawson is a global authority on knots who has been producing commercial ropework for over 50 years. He has written several books on the subject of knots and ropework and is a co-founder of the International Guild of Knot Tyers. He has been awarded an MBE for his contribution to the knot and rope industry.

www.despawson.com

Author's Acknowledgments

Putting this book together has been a team effort, not just by the team at DK and at the photographic studio, but by all those people who, over the centuries, have tied knots and shown them to others, so they are still known today. Many thanks to the members, past and present, of the International Guild of Knot Tyers who have stimulated me to develop my knowledge. I have also been lucky in the support and encouragement of my wife Liz who has enabled me to follow my dream as a ropeworker. To all these people, a big thank you.

Publisher's Acknowledgments

Dorling Kindersley would like to thank Dynamo for their time and assistance. DK would also like to thank Gareth Jones, Hugo Wilkinson, Lee Wilson and Maisie Peppitt for their editorial help and Michael Duffy, Phil Gamble, Peter Laws, Hannah Moore, Yenmai Tsang, Daksheeta Pattni and Vikram Singh for their design assistance. Thanks also to Nicholas Brewer for his help with the photography, and further thanks to Liza Bilal for modelling. DK India would like to thank Suchismita Banerjee, Manisha Jain, Tanya Mehrota, Neha Ruth Samuel, and Malavika Talukder.

The publisher would like to thank the following for their kind permission to reproduce their photographs:

(Key: a-above; b-below/bottom; c-centre; f-far; l-left; r-right; t-top)
Alamy Images: fc2 / picturesbyrob 189b; **Corbis:** Bill Holden / cultura 218, Eyecandy Images / Alloy 304b, Roy Morsch / Flirt 276-277b; **Dreamstime.com:** Ildipapp 186; **Getty Images:** Chel Beeson / Photolibrary 302, Jupiterimages / Comstock Images 370, Echo / Cultura 127b, Evan Sklar / Botanica 220-221b, Indeed / Taxi Japan 274, Ascent Xmedia / The Image Bank 166-167b
Jacket images: Front: **Corbis:** Shift Foto
All other images © Dorling Kindersley
For further information see: www.dkimages.com

International Guild of Knot Tyers

If you are interested in learning more about knots and ropework, the International Guild of Knot Tyers (www.igkt.net) offers a wealth of information and resources, and can put you in touch with fellow enthusiasts from the knot-tying community around the world.